Shaping Tomorrow

The Power of
Response Over
Circumstance

Ine Velaers

Copyright

This book is a work of fiction. Names, characters, places, and incidents either are products of the author's imagination or are used fictitiously. Any resemblance to actual persons, living or dead, events, or locales is entirely coincidental.

Copyright © 2024 Ine Velaers.

Cover design by Ine Velaers Artwork by Ine Velaers

Published by AdminVanguard

AdminVanguard Publishing supports the right to free expression and the fundamental value of copyright as it encourages writers, artists, and creators to produce the innovative and vital works that enhance and shape our culture.

For permission to use material from this book, please contact ine@innovinkcreations.com

Print: 978-2-9594459-0-3 Digital: 978-2-9594459-1-01

Printed in France

First Edition: July 2024

Table of Contents

Chapter 1

Harnessing Inner Strength: Embracing the Philosophy of Personal Power

In the journey of life, we often find ourselves at crossroads, faced with challenges that seem insurmountable. It's in these moments that the true essence of our character is revealed—not by the obstacles we encounter, but by how we choose to respond to them. This is the heart of "Shaping Tomorrow: The Power of Response Over Circumstance," a philosophy that champions the incredible strength of personal power.

Personal power is more than just a concept; it's a transformative approach to life. It's about understanding that while we may not have control over every situation that unfolds, we do hold the reins to our responses. This realization opens a gateway to a life lived with intention, resilience, and an empowering sense of agency.

Consider for a moment the various challenges you've faced in your own life. Whether they stemmed from personal relationships, professional setbacks, or internal battles, it's not the events themselves that define us, but rather our reactions to them. Our narrative is not scripted by the external world, but authored by our perceptions, decisions, and actions.

This journey of self-empowerment begins with a simple yet profound shift in mindset. It's about moving away from a place of blame or victimhood and stepping into a role where you are the architect of your own destiny. It's a transition from asking "Why is this happening to me?" to declaring "How can I grow from this?"

Each chapter of this book is designed not just to share insights but to invite you into a conversation. Through relatable stories and real-life examples, we explore the diverse ways individuals have harnessed their personal power to overcome adversity. These narratives are not just stories; they are mirrors reflecting the potential within each of us to rise above our circumstances.

But this book is more than just a collection of stories; it's a practical guide to cultivating your inner strength. We delve into strategies and exercises that encourage self-awareness, resilience, and proactive decision-making. These tools are not just theoretical but are meant to be applied, offering a pathway to transform insights into action.

As you embark on this journey, remember that personal power is not a destination but a continual process of growth and evolution. It requires patience, compassion for oneself, and the courage to face one's fears and vulnerabilities. It's about embracing the full spectrum of the human experience, recognizing that even in moments of doubt or despair, there lies an opportunity for growth and enlightenment.

"Shaping Tomorrow" is more than just a book; it's a companion on your journey towards a more empowered and fulfilling life. It's an invitation to break free from the chains of circumstance and step into a realm where you are the master of your destiny. Let's embark on this journey together, with open hearts and minds, ready to embrace the power of response over circumstance, and in doing so, shape a tomorrow that resonates with strength, hope, and endless possibilities.

Embracing Your Power: A Journey Through Life's Challenges

In the heart of France, where the spirit of resilience and the charm of life's simplicities blend seamlessly, there's a profound understanding that life's challenges are not just obstacles, but opportunities. This understanding forms the core of our journey in embracing personal power, a concept that transcends cultural boundaries and speaks to a universal human experience.

Personal power is often misconceived as a force exerted over others. However, it's truly about the strength we harness within ourselves, particularly when navigating life's inevitable challenges. It's a power that doesn't roar in defiance but whispers a gentle reminder: you are the sculptor of your destiny, not merely a bystander.

Imagine, for a moment, standing at the banks of the Seine on a misty morning, watching the river flow steadily. The water's journey, with its ebbs and flows, mirrors our own. Just as the Seine continues its course despite the rocks and curves, our path through life is marked by our ability to persist, adapt, and grow through our experiences.

This concept of personal power is not just theoretical; it's deeply practical and rooted in everyday life. Whether you're facing professional setbacks, personal dilemmas, or internal conflicts, the way you respond to these situations can transform your journey. It's about moving from a reactive stance, where situations control your emotions and decisions, to a proactive approach, where you consciously choose your responses.

Consider the story of a baker in a small French village, whose family bakery faced closure. Rather than succumbing to despair, she reimagined her approach, blending traditional recipes with innovative flavors. Her bakery not only survived but thrived, becoming a symbol of resilience and adaptability. This story reflects personal power in action: the ability to turn challenges into stepping stones.

In embracing this power, it's essential to connect with your inner self. Reflect on your experiences, the decisions you've made, and how they've shaped your journey. Personal power grows through self-awareness and the understanding that while we cannot control every aspect of life, we can control how we respond to it.

As you embark on this journey of self-discovery and empowerment, remember to approach each challenge with empathy for yourself and others. Each obstacle is a lesson in disguise, an opportunity to grow stronger, wiser, and more resilient. It's about finding harmony between accepting what cannot be changed and changing what you can.

In conclusion, personal power is not about dominance, but about embracing your inner strength and using it to navigate the complexities of life. It's a journey that requires courage, self-reflection, and a willingness to grow. Just like the enduring beauty of France, your journey through life's challenges can be a testament to the enduring power of the human spirit, a power that resides within each of us, waiting to be discovered and embraced.

Mindscapes: Navigating Life's Storms Through the Power of Thought"

In the realm of life's complexities, our mindset is like a compass, guiding us through the turbulent seas of challenges and difficulties. At the heart of this exploration is a simple, yet profound truth: the way we perceive difficulties shapes our response to them. Our mindsets aren't just passive observers; they actively construct our reality. When faced with a challenge, it's not just the situation itself that matters, but how we interpret and react to it.

Let's consider a scenario: two individuals face a similar setback at work. One sees it as a devastating blow, a confirmation of inadequacy. The other views it as an opportunity for growth, a stepping stone to greater understanding and skill. The same event, but through different mindsets, leads to vastly different outcomes. This is the power of perspective – it shapes our emotions, decisions, and ultimately, our life's trajectory.

In navigating through these mental landscapes, empathy and understanding are our allies. It's essential to approach our challenges with a sense of compassion, both for ourselves and others. Recognizing that difficulties are a universal part of the human experience allows us to face them with a sense of solidarity and shared humanity. Whether it's the bustling streets of Paris or the quiet countryside, challenges are a common thread in the tapestry of life.

However, cultivating a constructive mindset is not about dismissing the gravity of our struggles. It's about acknowledging them and consciously choosing how we respond. This book offers practical tools and exercises to help you reflect, reframe, and rebuild your mindset. These strategies are more than just theoretical concepts; they're actionable steps that you can integrate into your daily life.

Moreover, embracing a positive mindset doesn't mean turning a blind eye to reality. It's about finding balance –

acknowledging the storms while seeking the rainbow that follows. It's a journey of self-discovery, where you learn to harness the power of your thoughts to create a more resilient and empowered self.

As we journey through the chapters of this book, we'll explore stories from diverse backgrounds, each illustrating the transformative power of mindset. From the alleys of Paris to the farthest corners of the globe, these narratives will resonate with a universal truth: our internal dialogue is a powerful catalyst for change.

Cultivating Resilience: The Art of Positive Reframing

In the chaos of life, our resilience acts as a vibrant thread, adding strength and color to our experiences. Resilience is not just about enduring challenges; it's about adapting and thriving amidst them. This chapter delves into the art of positive reframing, a skill that allows us to view challenges not as roadblocks but as opportunities for growth and learning.

Consider the resilience of a vineyard owner in the French countryside. Year after year, the vines face unpredictable weather, yet they adapt, grow, and eventually yield a bountiful harvest. Similarly, we too can cultivate resilience by adapting our mindset and approach to life's unpredictable weather.

Positive reframing involves shifting our focus from what we've lost or what's gone wrong to what can be gained from the experience. It's about looking for the silver lining, even in the darkest of clouds. This doesn't mean ignoring the pain or difficulty of a situation but rather choosing to focus on the potential for positive outcomes.

This book offers practical exercises to help you practice positive reframing. For instance, when faced with a challenge, try to list three potential positive outcomes or lessons you can learn from the experience. These exercises are designed to be simple yet powerful, helping you to gradually shift your perspective and cultivate a more resilient mindset.

Moreover, resilience is also about understanding our limitations and embracing self-compassion. It's about recognizing that being resilient doesn't mean being invincible. Sometimes, resilience means knowing when to take a step back, rest, and recharge.

Empowering Choices: Taking Control of Your Narrative

Life is a series of choices, and each choice we make shapes our narrative. In this chapter, we explore the empowering realization that while we may not control every aspect of our lives, we do control the choices we make. This understanding is a cornerstone of personal power.

Empowering choices are about taking proactive steps to shape our lives in alignment with our values and goals. It's about choosing how to respond to life's challenges, rather than being swept away by them. This concept is beautifully illustrated by the story of a Parisian artist who, despite facing criticism, chose to pursue her unique style, eventually gaining recognition for her authentic work.

This book provides you with strategies to make empowering choices. It includes exercises to help you identify your core values and align your choices with them. These exercises are not just about introspection but about taking concrete steps towards living a life that is true to who you are.

Moreover, making empowering choices also involves acknowledging and learning from past choices. It's about understanding that mistakes are not failures but stepping stones to wisdom and growth.

Journeying Towards Empowerment: The Final Motivation

As we bring this chapter to a close, it's important to reflect on the journey we've embarked upon together. "Harnessing Inner Strength: Embracing the Philosophy of Personal Power" is more than just a guide; it's a call to action, a beckoning towards a life of intentional living and empowerment.

The stories, examples, and strategies shared in these pages are not mere words but tools for transformation. They are the keys to unlocking a life of resilience, growth, and personal power. This book is an invitation to step into a world where challenges are met with courage, where setbacks become springboards for growth, and where every day is an opportunity to write a new page in the story of your life.

As you move forward from this chapter, carry with you the knowledge that the power to shape your destiny lies within your hands. Each decision you make, each reaction you choose, weaves the fabric of your future. Remember, the challenges you face are not barriers, but stepping stones to a higher version of yourself.

Embrace this journey with an open heart and a willing spirit. Let the stories of resilience inspire you, let the strategies guide you, and let your personal power propel you. You have the strength to overcome, the wisdom to grow, and the courage to soar.

As you close this chapter and look towards the next, do so with a renewed sense of purpose and determination. Know that you are capable, you are resilient, and you are empowered. Your journey towards personal power is just beginning, and the path ahead is filled with limitless possibilities.

Step forward with confidence, embrace the lessons life offers, and shape your tomorrow with the strength of your today. The journey of personal power is not just about reaching a destination; it's about savoring each step, learning from each stumble, and celebrating each triumph.

Remember, in the grand tapestry of life, you are the artist, and every stroke of resilience, every hue of courage, adds depth and beauty to your masterpiece. So, go forth with conviction, shape your narrative with bold strokes, and let your journey of empowerment be your greatest work of art.

Chapter 2

Healing from Yesterday: Embracing Growth Beyond a Troubled Past

In "Shaping Tomorrow: The Power of Response Over Circumstance," we embark on a crucial chapter of our journey: understanding and healing from the legacy of a troubled past. The shadows cast by our previous experiences often shape our present, influencing our reactions, decisions, and our perception of the world. This chapter, "Healing from Yesterday: Embracing Growth Beyond a Troubled Past," delves into the intricate process of acknowledging, understanding, and ultimately growing from our past struggles.

Understanding the Echoes of the Past

The past, with its complexities and challenges, leaves an indelible mark on our lives. For many, it's a tapestry woven with threads of trials, tribulations, and sometimes traumas that can influence the present in profound ways. Recognizing this influence is the first step towards healing. It involves a compassionate exploration of our history, identifying the experiences that have shaped us, and acknowledging their impact on our current life.

Creating a Dialogue with Our History

In this journey of healing, the power of storytelling emerges as a vital tool. By sharing relatable stories of individuals who have navigated their way through the aftermath of a troubled past, we create a space for empathy and understanding. These narratives are not just tales of struggle but are beacons of hope, illustrating the incredible resilience of the human spirit. They remind us that our past does not define us; rather, it's our response to it that shapes our future.

The Path to Empowerment: Learning from Our Experiences

A troubled past can often make us feel trapped, leading to a sense of victimhood. However, this chapter guides readers through shifting this perspective. It's about moving from a state of feeling acted upon by our past to a position where we actively learn from and use these experiences as a foundation for growth. Practical advice, reflections, and exercises are provided to encourage this shift, helping readers to not only understand their past but also to reclaim their narrative.

Fostering Self-Compassion and Understanding

One of the most critical aspects of dealing with a troubled past is practicing self-compassion. This chapter emphasizes the importance of being kind to oneself, acknowledging that healing is a journey, not a destination. It encourages readers to view their past struggles not as a source of shame but as a testament to their strength and resilience.

Transforming Pain into Power

The ultimate goal of this chapter is to empower readers to transform their past pain into a source of strength. This transformation is not about erasing the past but about changing our relationship with it. It's about finding meaning in our experiences and using them to fuel our growth and resilience.

Echoes of a Troubled Childhood: Understanding and Healing

In the intricate journey of life, the experiences of our childhood cast long shadows into our adult lives, shaping our thoughts, behaviors, and emotional responses.

Navigating the Complexities of a Difficult Family Environment

The story of a person growing up in a troubled family environment is a complex one, marked by a myriad of challenges. These challenges can range from facing neglect or emotional unavailability from parents, to enduring a household filled with conflict and instability. For many, such an environment becomes the backdrop of their formative years, deeply influencing their sense of self and their view of the world.

In this context, the person may grapple with feelings of insecurity, develop a deep-seated need for approval, or struggle with establishing healthy boundaries in relationships. The lack of a nurturing and stable environment can leave them feeling isolated and unsupported, impacting their ability to form secure and trusting relationships later in life.

The Psychological Impact of a Troubled Childhood

The psychological impact of growing up in such an environment is profound. It often leads to a complex interplay of emotions and behaviors that can persist well into adulthood. This can manifest in various ways – from difficulties in trusting others and chronic self-doubt to more severe issues like anxiety and depression.

These psychological echoes of a troubled childhood are not just fleeting memories; they are deeply embedded experiences that shape an individual's approach to life. They can influence how one handles stress, their self-esteem, and even their approach to parenting.

A Journey of Understanding and Empathy

Through compassionate storytelling and examples, this chapter aims to bridge a connection with readers who may have experienced similar challenges. By sharing these stories, it opens a dialogue that is not only empathetic but also inclusive, ensuring that no reader feels alone in their experience.

It's crucial to approach this sensitive topic with care and empathy. The goal is not to dwell on the pain of the past, but to offer understanding and support. Acknowledging these struggles is the first step in a healing journey that many embark upon.

Towards Healing and Growth

Healing from the scars of a troubled childhood is not a linear process; it's a path marked with its own set of challenges and triumphs. This chapter provides actionable advice to aid in this healing process, including exercises for self-reflection and personal growth. These activities are designed to encourage readers to delve into their past, understand its impact, and gradually work towards a healthier, more empowered self.

Rewriting the Script: From Childhood Challenges to Adult Triumphs

The journey from a troubled childhood to a thriving adulthood is akin to navigating a complex labyrinth. It's a path riddled with obstacles, yet it holds the potential for profound transformation. This chapter delves into the psychological impact of a challenging childhood and its ripple effects on adult relationships. We'll explore how the scars of the past can shape, but not define, our future relationships and decision-making.

Growing up in an unstable or neglectful environment can leave deep-seated marks on a person's psyche. Children who face such adversity often develop survival mechanisms that, while necessary in their youth, can become hindrances in adulthood. The instinct to shield oneself, to mistrust, or to fear abandonment can seep into adult relationships, sometimes sabotaging them before they even begin.

But here's the powerful truth: the past does not have to dictate your future. Every day presents a new opportunity for change, a chance to make a decision that alters the course of your life. It's about harnessing the power of small, yet significant choices. Every time you confront a fear, every moment you choose trust over suspicion, you're rewriting your story.

Consider the case of John, a friend of mine. He grew up in a home where emotional expression was frowned upon, leading him to bottle up his feelings. As an adult, this manifested in his inability to form deep, meaningful relationships. The breakthrough came when he decided to seek therapy. That single decision, that small step towards understanding himself, revolutionized his approach to relationships. It wasn't an overnight change, but a gradual evolution, proving that the journey of a thousand miles begins with a single step.

This principle applies to all aspects of life. The impact of a troubled childhood on adult relationships is significant, but it's not insurmountable. It's about recognizing patterns, understanding their origins, and consciously choosing a different path.

Embracing vulnerability, seeking support, and practicing self-awareness are steps in this transformative journey. They are decisions that, though small, wield the power to redirect the trajectory of your life. It's about shifting from a passive acceptance of your past to an active shaping of your future.

This path isn't easy, and it's often uncomfortable, but growth lies in discomfort. By facing your fears and challenging your ingrained habits, you're not only improving your relationships but also empowering yourself. You're taking control, proving that you are not a product of your past, but a creator of your future.

The psychological impact of a troubled childhood is a reality for many, but it doesn't have to be a life sentence. The correlation between these early experiences and adult relationships is undeniable, but so is the power of choice and change. By making small, conscious decisions every day, you can reshape your life's narrative. Remember, in the script of your life, you are the writer, the director, and the star. It's time to take control and craft a story of resilience, empowerment, and triumph.

Breaking the Mold: Redefining Love and Trust

In a world brimming with stereotypes and misconceptions about love and trust, it's easy to find ourselves trapped in a cycle of unrealistic expectations and disillusionment. This chapter is about breaking free from those molds, about redefining what love and trust truly mean in our lives. It's about understanding that the most empowering thing we can do is to take control of our perceptions and responses in relationships.

The first misconception we often encounter is the idea that love and trust are things that just happen to us, like rain falling from the sky. The reality, however, is far more proactive. Love and trust are choices, commitments we make and actions we take every single day. They are not static states of being but dynamic processes that evolve with time and effort.

Let's consider trust. We've been led to believe that trust is something that, once broken, is nearly impossible to rebuild. But here's a different perspective: trust is like a muscle. The more you work on it, the stronger it becomes. It's about making the decision to try again, to open yourself up to the possibility of being hurt but also to the potential of deeper connection.

Now, let's talk about love. How often have we heard that love should be easy and effortless? This notion sets us up for failure. Real love is about showing up, even when it's hard. It's about choosing to love someone, warts and all. It's about understanding that love is not just a feeling, but an action.

I learned this the hard way through a personal experience. A few years back, I faced a rough patch in my marriage. We had fallen into the trap of taking each other for granted. It was only when we both made the conscious decision to work on our relationship, to actively show love and rebuild trust, that things began to change. It required effort, patience, and a lot of honest conversations, but it was worth it.

Remember, overcoming stereotypes and misconceptions is not just about changing how we view love and trust; it's also about changing how we act on them. It's about making small, deliberate choices that align with this new understanding. It could be as simple as expressing gratitude, listening actively, or being open about your vulnerabilities.

This journey requires resilience and a willingness to challenge long-held beliefs. But the empowerment that comes from taking control of your love life and trust dynamics is immeasurable. You're no longer a passive participant in your relationships; you're an active architect, crafting connections that are authentic and fulfilling.

Challenge the stereotypes and misconceptions you hold about love and trust. Make the conscious decision to approach them differently, to build them actively in your relationships. Embrace the idea that through small, daily decisions, you have the power to redefine these concepts in your life, leading to more genuine and satisfying connections. Remember, in the grand narrative of your life, you hold the pen, and it's time to write a story of love and trust that truly resonates with who you are.

Charting a New Course: Strategies for Healing from a Difficult Past

Healing from a difficult past isn't just about moving on; it's about moving forward with intention and strength. It's a journey that requires courage, resilience, and a series of deliberate decisions that propel you towards a future of your own making. This chapter is dedicated to unpacking practical strategies for healing and transcending the constraints of a painful history. It's about empowering you to take the reins of your life, transforming your past into a foundation for growth and success.

Let's start with the most crucial step: acknowledging the past. Acknowledging doesn't mean dwelling on the pain or allowing it to define you. It means recognizing the experiences that have shaped you and understanding their impact. This recognition is empowering. It's the first step in reclaiming control over your life narrative.

Once you've acknowledged your past, the next step is to understand that healing is not a linear process. There will be setbacks, and that's okay. Healing is not about reaching a destination; it's about growing through the journey. Be kind to yourself in this process. Patience and self-compassion are your allies here.

Now, let's talk about one of the most transformative strategies: reframing your story. You can't change the past, but you can change how you view it. Instead of seeing your past experiences as solely negative, look for the strength and resilience they have instilled in you. This shift in perspective isn't about sugarcoating the past; it's about recognizing that even in pain, there is potential for growth.

For instance, I once met someone who had overcome a tumultuous childhood. Instead of allowing his past to engulf him in bitterness, he used it to fuel his passion for helping others. He became a counselor, using his experiences to empathize and guide others through their struggles. His past didn't hold him back; it propelled him forward.

Another vital strategy is building a support system. Surround yourself with people who uplift and understand you. Healing is not a journey you have to take alone. The right support system can provide the strength and perspective needed when the going gets tough.

Additionally, cultivating self-awareness is key. Understand your triggers and learn how to manage them. This might involve therapy, journaling, or mindfulness practices. The goal is to develop a deep understanding of yourself, so you can navigate your emotions and reactions in a healthy, constructive way.

Finally, take action. Healing requires more than just introspection; it requires tangible steps. Set small, achievable goals that align with your vision for the future. These steps, no matter how small, are significant. They are the building blocks of a new life, one that you are actively shaping.

Healing from a difficult past is about rewriting your story. It's about making conscious decisions that align with who you want to be and the life you want to live. Remember, you are not defined by your past, but by the actions you take and the choices you make in the present. Embrace your journey with courage and conviction, and know that every step forward is a step towards a brighter, self-empowered future.

Triumphs in the City of Lights: Overcoming Adversity in France

In the journey of life, the most inspiring stories often come from those who have faced and overcome incredible adversities. This chapter celebrates the resilience and empowerment of individuals in France who have turned their challenging backgrounds into powerful narratives of success. Their stories are not just tales of survival; they are beacons of hope and testament to the power of decision-making and the impact of small, consistent changes.

First, let's visit the story of Clara, a young woman from the outskirts of Paris. Growing up in a low-income neighborhood, Clara faced the stereotypes and limitations often imposed by society. But instead of succumbing to these, she used them as fuel. With a passion for art, she started painting, using the walls of her neighborhood as her canvas. Her art, vibrant and full of life, caught the attention of a local gallery owner. Today, Clara is a celebrated artist, showcasing the beauty and complexity of her world through her work. Her journey illustrates that where you come from doesn't have to dictate where you're going. It's the small steps, the daily grind, and the unwavering belief in oneself that pave the way to success.

Then there's the story of Louis, a young man from Lyon, who overcame a tumultuous childhood marked by family instability. Despite his rocky start, Louis made a decisive choice to pursue his education. He spent nights studying by the dim light of his room, determined to change his narrative. His perseverance paid off when he earned a scholarship to a prestigious university. Now a successful engineer, Louis mentors young people from similar backgrounds, inspiring them to dream big and work hard.

These stories are not anomalies; they're proof of the incredible potential that lies within each of us to rise above our circumstances. They embody the essence of taking control, of making deliberate choices that shape our destinies. It's about recognizing that while we can't control where we come from, we have absolute power over where we go.

The common thread in these stories is the power of decision-making. Each of these individuals faced a moment where they had to decide whether to be defined by their past or to define their future. They chose the latter, making small, strategic changes that collectively transformed their lives.

In essence, their journeys mirror the concept of the '5 Second Rule' in action—making swift, decisive moves that pivot their life's trajectory. It's about the courage to take that first step, the resilience to keep going, and the wisdom to know that every small step counts.

As we draw inspiration from Clara, Louis, and many others, let their stories be a reminder that you, too, have the power to rewrite your narrative. No matter what your background is, you have the capacity to create a future that reflects your aspirations and dreams. It's about taking that first step, then another, and another, until you look back and realize how far you've come. Remember, in the grand tapestry of life, every thread you weave, no matter how small, contributes to the masterpiece that is your life story.

Embracing the Horizon: Sealing Your Journey with Hope and Action

As we draw this chapter to a close, it's time to turn our reflections into resolutions, our insights into actions. This journey you've embarked upon, filled with stories of resilience and transformation, is not just about understanding; it's about doing. It's about embracing the horizon of your life with hope and a proactive spirit.

Every story you've encountered in these pages, every piece of advice, converges to this singular truth: You have the power to shape your destiny. Your past, no matter how challenging, is a chapter, not the whole story. The pen is in your hands, and the pages ahead are blank, waiting for you to script your triumph.

First and foremost, believe in your ability to change. This belief is the cornerstone of all transformation. It's the fuel that powers your journey. Even on days when this belief wavers, remember the stories of those who walked this path before you. Let their victories reignite your faith in your potential.

Next, set your intentions. What is it that you want to achieve? Where do you see yourself in the next year, five years, or ten years? Be specific, be bold. These intentions are your guiding stars, illuminating the path towards your goals.

Now, translate these intentions into actionable steps. Break down your goals into smaller, manageable tasks. Remember, change doesn't happen overnight. It's the result of small, consistent efforts. Each step you take, no matter how small, is a step closer to your desired future.

Along this journey, cultivate a mindset of resilience. You will encounter obstacles, but it's your response to these challenges that defines your journey. Every setback is an opportunity to learn, to grow, and to come back stronger.

Don't forget to build a support system. Surround yourself with people who believe in you, who encourage your dreams, and who are there to lift you up when you falter. We are social beings, and the company we keep can significantly influence our path.

Most importantly, practice self-compassion. Be kind to yourself during this journey. Celebrate your victories, no matter how small, and forgive yourself for the setbacks. Growth is a process, and kindness towards oneself is a vital part of it.

As we conclude, remember that the horizon is always expanding, always inviting you to explore new possibilities and adventures. Your journey doesn't end here. It's a continuous, evolving path where every step counts, every decision matters, and every dream is valid.

Embrace your horizon with hope, armed with the knowledge that you are capable, resilient, and empowered. You are the author of your story, the master of your journey, and the architect of your destiny. Go forth with confidence and conviction, and make your mark on the world.

Chapter 3

Beyond Blame: Owning Our Present

In the medley of life, it's easy to get entangled in the threads of the past, especially when they are woven with hurt, regret, or disappointment. But here's the empowering truth: the present is yours to shape. This chapter, "Beyond Blame: Owning Our Present," is about taking that crucial step from assigning blame for our current circumstances to taking ownership of them. It's about embracing the power within us to change our story, one decision, one action at a time.

The habit of blaming is deeply ingrained in many of us. We blame our upbringing, our socio-economic background, our bad luck, or even other people for where we are in life.

While these factors undoubtedly influence our journey, they don't control it. The steering wheel is in your hands, and it's time to take the driver's seat.

Let's start with a reality check: Blame is a comfort zone. It's easier to point fingers than to confront our own role in our current reality. But comfort zones are breeding grounds for stagnation. The moment we stop blaming and start owning our situations, that's when true growth begins. It's uncomfortable, yes, but remember, comfort never led to greatness.

Imagine this: you're stuck in a job you don't love, blaming the economy, your bad luck, or your lack of connections. Now, flip the script. What if, instead of blame, you focus on what you can control? Your skills, your network, your mindset. Start with small steps - a course to enhance your skills, reaching out to people in your desired industry, or simply shifting your attitude towards your current job. These are small changes, but their impact on your life trajectory can be monumental.

Personal anecdotes are powerful, so let me share one. I once knew a woman, Sarah, who blamed her unfulfilling relationships on her troubled childhood. It was a narrative deeply rooted in her psyche. The turning point came when she decided to take ownership of her happiness. She began by setting boundaries, understanding her worth, and seeking therapy. This shift from blame to ownership didn't change her past, but it completely transformed her future.

This process of owning your present is not about ignoring the impact of past experiences. It's about shifting from a mindset of helplessness to one of empowerment. It's about recognizing that while we can't change the past, we have immense power over our present and future.

Owning your present also involves embracing responsibility – not just for your actions, but also for your reactions, emotions, and decisions. It's about acknowledging that your life is a reflection of the choices you make every day. Each decision, no matter how small, is a brick in the foundation of your life.

As we move forward, let's hold onto this empowering realization: You are not a passive spectator in your life; you are the lead actor. The script may have been influenced by various factors, but you have the creative license to rewrite it. Start with today, with this moment. Own it, shape it, and watch as the pages of your life unfold in a direction that reflects your true potential and desires.

Moving beyond blame to owning our present is a journey of empowerment, courage, and transformation. It's about recognizing that the power to change our story lies within us, in the decisions we make, the actions we take, and the mindset we adopt. Embrace this journey with an open heart and a willing spirit, and step into a future where you are the master of your destiny.

Unraveling the Blame Game: Understanding Our Psychological Ties to the Past

Our upbringing often leads the first few steps. This chapter delves into a territory we've all navigated: the tendency to blame our upbringing for the challenges we face today. It's a natural inclination, rooted in the very fabric of our psychological makeup, but it's also a chain that can be broken. Here, we'll explore the psychological basis for this blame game, and more importantly, how we can move beyond it to take control of our narratives.

The psychological inclination to blame our upbringing for current issues is not without merit. Our formative years are like the programming phase of our life's computer, laying down the foundational operating system – beliefs, habits, and emotional responses. When these early experiences are fraught with negativity or trauma, they can leave lasting impressions, influencing our adult behaviors and attitudes.

This blame, however, while understandable, can become a crutch, a reason to avoid personal growth. It's comfortable to point to the past as the reason for our current struggles – it absolves us of immediate responsibility. But here's the empowering twist: acknowledging the influence of our past without letting it dictate our present is where true growth begins.

Consider the story of Alex, who always felt overshadowed by his siblings, leading to a deep-seated belief that he was not good enough. As an adult, this manifested in a fear of taking risks and asserting himself. It was only when he recognized this pattern and its roots that he was able to challenge it. He began to take small but significant steps, like voicing his opinions in meetings and taking on projects that scared him. These actions, seemingly small, were monumental in rewriting his self-perception.

It's crucial to understand that our brains are wired to make sense of our experiences, and this often means drawing a straight line from past to present. This is not just a psychological phenomenon; it's a survival mechanism. It helps us navigate our world by creating a narrative that explains our current circumstances. But, and here's the key, we are not bound by this narrative.

Breaking free from this pattern involves a conscious decision to reframe our perspective. It's about recognizing the lessons from our past and using them as stepping stones, not stumbling blocks. It's about replacing blame with empowerment, recognizing that while we cannot change our history, we can shape our destiny.

This shift requires action. It's not enough to simply understand the influence of our past; we must actively work to create a new narrative. This can be through therapy, self-reflection, challenging our limiting beliefs, and most importantly, making different choices – choices that reflect who we want to be, not who our past has conditioned us to be.

While our upbringing undoubtedly shapes us, it does not define us. The psychological basis for blaming our past is a starting point for understanding, but the journey doesn't end there. It's a springboard into a process of self-discovery and empowerment. Every day presents a new opportunity to make choices that align with our desired future, not our past experiences. Embrace this journey with courage and an open heart, and watch as you transform not just your narrative, but your life.

Shifting Blame, Shaping Growth: Navigating Towards Personal Fulfillment

The game of blame is as old as humanity itself, yet its impact on personal growth and happiness remains a compelling story of our times. This chapter is not just about understanding the dynamics of external blame; it's about transcending it, about realizing that the key to our growth and happiness lies within us, not outside. It's about the power of decision-making and embracing small changes that can significantly alter our life's trajectory.

Blaming external factors for our shortcomings or unhappiness is a common defense mechanism. It's easy, convenient, and it absolves us of immediate responsibility. But what happens when we consistently blame others or our circumstances? We hand over our power, our agency to shape our lives. We become mere spectators in our own story, watching life unfold rather than actively steering its course.

The truth is, every time we point a finger outward, we miss an opportunity to look inward and grow. Personal growth thrives in the soil of self-reflection and responsibility. When we shift from external blame to internal accountability, we unlock a powerful mechanism for change.

Let's consider a real-life example. I once met a man named Tom, who constantly blamed his job and boss for his unhappiness. He believed his lack of career progression was entirely due to external factors. It wasn't until Tom took a hard look at himself and recognized his own role in the situation - his reluctance to seek new opportunities, his fear of change - that things began to shift. He started taking courses to improve his skills, networked within his industry, and soon, he landed a role that reignited his passion. This change began with a shift in perspective - from blame to self-empowerment.

External blame is not just a barrier to personal growth; it's a thief of happiness. Happiness that's contingent on external validation or circumstances is fragile and fleeting. True, lasting happiness comes from within - from a sense of personal accomplishment, self-acceptance, and the empowerment that comes with taking control of one's life.

Breaking free from the cycle of external blame requires conscious effort. It starts with acknowledging that while we may not control every aspect of our lives, we control our reactions and decisions. It's about focusing on what we can change - our attitudes, our efforts, our mindset.

Small, consistent steps lead to significant changes. Start by identifying areas in your life where you've been playing the blame game. Then, ask yourself, "What can I do differently?" It could be as simple as changing your approach to a problem, seeking feedback for personal improvement, or shifting your mindset from victimhood to agency.

The impact of external blame on personal growth and happiness cannot be overstated. It's a barrier that keeps us from realizing our full potential. The journey towards personal fulfillment involves moving beyond blame and taking ownership of our lives. Remember, the most empowering moment in your life is when you realize that your growth, your happiness, your future, is in your hands. Make the decision today to shift from blame to self-empowerment, and watch as your life transforms in the most extraordinary ways.

From Blame to Empowerment: Steering Your Life with Purpose

Blame is a familiar road for many of us, a path we tread when things don't go as planned. It's easy to fall into the trap of blaming circumstances, other people, or even ourselves when faced with challenges. But there's a more empowering route available, one that leads to growth, resilience, and genuine happiness. This chapter is about making that critical shift from blame to empowerment, transforming how we navigate life's ups and downs.

Blame is like quicksand; the more we indulge in it, the deeper we sink, rendering ourselves powerless. It's a passive stance, where we see ourselves as victims of our circumstances. However, the moment we shift our focus to empowerment, we begin to see challenges as opportunities for growth. This shift is not just motivational rhetoric; it's a practical approach to life that encourages proactive problem-solving and personal responsibility.

Think about a time when something didn't go your way. Maybe you missed a job promotion or had a falling out with a friend. It's natural to initially react with blame. But what happens when you pause and ask yourself, "What can I learn from this? What's in my control to change?" This change in perspective is the first step towards empowerment.

Let me share a story to illustrate this point. Sarah, a friend of mine, was constantly upset about her strained relationship with her sister, often blaming her sister's attitude for their issues. After many heart-to-hearts, Sarah decided to shift her approach. She began focusing on how she could contribute to a better relationship, initiating open conversations and setting boundaries. This didn't change her sister overnight, but it transformed their dynamic gradually. Sarah felt more in control and less victimized by the situation.

Empowerment also means embracing the idea that we are the architects of our own lives. It's recognizing that while we cannot control everything that happens to us, we have the power to control our responses. This realization is liberating. It shifts our mindset from one of helplessness to one of strength and possibility.

Another key aspect of moving from blame to empowerment is letting go of the need for external validation. So often, our blame is rooted in not meeting the expectations of others, or society at large. Empowerment comes from setting and living by your own standards, values, and goals.

It's important to acknowledge that this shift doesn't happen overnight. It's a process that requires practice and patience. Start small: identify one area of your life where you've been playing the blame game. Then, consciously work towards shifting your mindset. Ask yourself empowering questions, explore different responses, and take actionable steps towards change.

Shifting focus from blame to empowerment is a transformative journey. It's about taking ownership of your life, your decisions, and your happiness. This shift doesn't mean you won't face challenges, but it ensures you face them with a mindset that fosters resilience, growth, and fulfillment. Remember, in the story of your life, you're not just the main character; you're also the writer. Write a story of empowerment, purpose, and relentless pursuit of your potential.

Mastering the Self: Techniques for Developing Self-Awareness and Accountability

In the journey of self-improvement, two vital companions are self-awareness and accountability. They are the cornerstones of personal growth, guiding us towards a deeper understanding of ourselves and fostering a sense of responsibility for our actions. This chapter focuses on practical techniques for cultivating these qualities, empowering you to become the master of your destiny.

Self-awareness is like holding a mirror to your soul; it's about understanding your thoughts, emotions, and behaviors. It's the first step in recognizing your strengths and areas for improvement. But how do we develop this crucial skill?

Start with reflection. Dedicate time each day to introspect. It could be through journaling, meditation, or simply sitting quietly and pondering your day. Ask yourself questions like, "Why did I react that way in that situation?" or "What are my core values and are my actions aligning with them?" This process of self-inquiry helps peel back the layers, revealing your true self.

Another powerful tool is feedback. Seek it out from friends, family, and colleagues. It can be eye-opening to see yourself from another's perspective. But remember, it's not about taking every piece of feedback to heart; it's about evaluating it against your own understanding of yourself and taking what's useful.

Now, let's talk about accountability. It's easy to make promises to ourselves, but how often do we keep them? Accountability is about owning your commitments and taking responsibility for your actions, especially when no one else is watching.

One effective technique is to set clear, measurable goals. Write them down and break them into smaller tasks. It's not just about setting goals; it's about following through. Track your progress regularly. This habit not only keeps you accountable but also provides a sense of achievement as you tick off each task.

Let me share a story to bring this to life. I once worked with someone, Emily, who struggled with time management. She would often miss deadlines and then blame external factors. We worked on developing her accountability. She started by setting daily goals, and every evening, she would review what she achieved against her plan. This simple practice transformed her work ethic. She became more productive, reliable, and, importantly, she felt more in control of her life.

A key component of developing accountability is embracing the power of small changes. Remember, Rome wasn't built in a day, and neither is personal growth. It's the small, consistent actions that add up to significant changes.

Lastly, practice resilience. You will face setbacks in your journey towards self-awareness and accountability. Embrace these as learning opportunities rather than failures. Each setback is a chance to understand yourself better and to reinforce your commitment to growth.

Developing self-awareness and accountability is a transformative journey. It requires honesty, commitment, and a willingness to step out of your comfort zone. Embrace these techniques with an open heart and a determined mind. Remember, the journey to mastering the self is ongoing, but with each step, you become more empowered, more in control, and more aligned with your true potential.

Owning the Now: Transformational Tales of Personal Triumph

The most powerful stories of transformation are those where individuals grasp the reins of their present, steering their lives towards success and fulfillment. This chapter celebrates the journeys of people who, by owning their present, have rewritten their destinies. These are not just tales of achievement; they're blueprints for personal empowerment and resilience.

One such story is of Maya, a marketing executive in a high-powered firm. On the surface, Maya had it all - a great career, a bustling social life, and the trappings of success. But beneath the surface, she was burning out. Her health and personal life were paying the price. The turning point came when Maya decided to take ownership of her present. She started by making small changes - prioritizing her health, setting boundaries at work, and carving out time for self-care. These changes, seemingly minor, had a profound impact. Maya not only improved her health and well-being but also became more effective at her job. By owning her present, she transformed her life into one of balance and genuine fulfillment.

Then there's the story of Carlos, who grew up in a challenging neighborhood, often finding himself on the wrong side of the law. Many wrote him off, expecting him to fall into a life of crime. But Carlos had a different vision for his life. He realized that his future was in his hands, and he decided to own his present. He went back to school, worked odd jobs to support himself, and, against all odds, earned a scholarship to college. Today, Carlos is a social worker, using his experiences to guide young people in similar situations. His story is a testament to the power of owning your present, regardless of your past.

These stories exemplify the incredible power of decision-making in shaping one's life trajectory. It's not just about making monumental choices; it's about the small, daily decisions that gradually steer your life in a new direction.

Owning your present means taking responsibility for your life as it is now, not as you wish it to be or as it used to be. It's about acknowledging your current situation, recognizing your power to change it, and then taking action. It's a process that requires courage, honesty, and resilience.

What these stories also highlight is the ripple effect of owning your present. When you start making changes in your life, it's not just your own life that transforms. You become an inspiration to others. Your story becomes a beacon of hope and a guide for those who might be struggling with their own challenges.

The success stories of Maya, Carlos, and countless others are powerful reminders of what we can achieve when we take control of our present. They teach us that no matter where we are in life, we have the power to change our course. It's about making the decision to act, to take that first step, and then the next. Remember, the journey of a thousand miles begins with a single step. Own your present, embrace your power, and watch as your life transforms into a story of success, happiness, and personal empowerment.

Chapter 4

Wisdom from Wounds: Embracing Life's Lessons

It goes without saying, the chapters we often wish to skip are those filled with challenges and setbacks. Yet, it is precisely these chapters that hold the most profound lessons. "Wisdom from Wounds" is about transforming our struggles into stepping stones for personal growth and empowerment. It's about seeing the wisdom hidden within our wounds, using them not as reasons to hold back but as catalysts to propel us forward.

Every wound, every struggle, carries with it a lesson. The key is to shift our perspective, to see these challenges as opportunities for growth and self-discovery. This shift is not about diminishing the pain or difficulty of our experiences but about extracting value from them.

Consider the story of Angela, who faced a series of professional setbacks. Each rejection, each failure, was a blow to her confidence. But instead of letting these experiences define her, Angela chose to learn from them. She analyzed her approaches, sought feedback, and identified areas for improvement. These setbacks became her greatest teachers, guiding her towards a more refined and effective career strategy. Today, Angela is thriving in her field, her success built on the foundations of her past 'failures'.

The wisdom we gain from our wounds is not just about personal achievements. It's also about developing empathy, resilience, and a deeper understanding of life. When we navigate through tough times, we emerge with a heightened sense of empathy for others facing similar challenges. Our struggles become a source of strength, not just for ourselves but for those around us.

One of the most empowering aspects of embracing our wounds is the realization that we have control over our reactions. We may not have control over what happens to us, but we always have control over how we respond. This is where the power of decision-making comes in. Choosing to respond to our challenges with a mindset of growth and learning is a conscious decision, one that can change the trajectory of our lives.

Small changes in our mindset and approach can have a significant impact. It's about taking those lessons and incorporating them into our daily lives. Whether it's being more mindful of our reactions, changing our approach to problem-solving, or simply being kinder to ourselves, these small shifts can lead to profound transformations.

Unveiling Strength: The Journey of Post-Traumatic Growth

In the landscape of human experience, trauma stands as a formidable mountain, its shadow often looming large over our lives. But there's a lesser-told story, one that speaks of the verdant valleys beyond this mountain – the story of post-traumatic growth. This chapter is dedicated to exploring this concept, to understanding how, from the depths of our struggles, we can rise with newfound strength, wisdom, and resilience.

Post-traumatic growth is not about glorifying suffering or diminishing the pain and complexity of traumatic experiences. It's about acknowledging the transformative power that can emerge in the aftermath of trauma. This growth manifests in various ways: a renewed appreciation for life, deeper personal relationships, a sense of increased personal strength, spiritual change, and the recognition of new possibilities or paths in life.

Take, for example, the story of Emma, a survivor of a serious car accident. In the months following her ordeal, Emma battled with fear, anxiety, and the physical challenges of recovery. However, through this journey, she discovered an inner resilience she never knew she had. She began to see life through a different lens, cherishing each moment with a depth of gratitude that was absent before her accident. Emma's story exemplifies the essence of post-traumatic growth – the discovery of personal strength and a profound appreciation for life, born out of the crucible of adversity.

The key to unlocking this growth lies in how we process and respond to our trauma. It requires an openness to self-reflection, a willingness to seek meaning and understanding in our experiences. This process is deeply personal and can vary greatly from one individual to another. For some, it might involve therapy or counseling, while for others, it might involve turning to art, spirituality, or community support.

It's important to remember that post-traumatic growth does not imply a smooth or easy journey. The road to recovery can be fraught with challenges and setbacks. Yet, it is through navigating these difficulties that growth occurs. It's about making a series of small decisions that gradually guide you towards healing and transformation.

One effective approach to fostering post-traumatic growth is to actively cultivate a positive outlook. This doesn't mean ignoring the pain or hardship of your experience. Rather, it's about acknowledging your pain and then deliberately seeking the silver linings. It's about asking yourself, "What can I learn from this? How has this experience shaped me for the better?"

Another critical aspect is the development of resilience. Resilience doesn't mean you don't feel the pain or grief that comes with trauma. It means you've developed the tools to navigate through it. Building resilience can involve practices like mindfulness, developing strong support networks, and engaging in activities that bring joy and fulfillment.

Post-traumatic growth offers a powerful counter-narrative to the idea that trauma leaves only destruction in its wake. It opens up a world where pain can be the catalyst for profound personal transformation. This chapter invites you to explore this concept, to find hope in the knowledge that even in our darkest moments, there's an opportunity for growth, strength, and renewal. As you journey through your own experiences, remember that within you lies an incredible capacity for resilience and transformation, a force that can turn the deepest wounds into wellsprings of wisdom and strength.

Resilience in the Heart of France: Lessons of Growth and Triumph

In the beautiful and diverse landscapes of France, from the bustling streets of Paris to the serene vineyards of Bordeaux, there are stories of resilience and growth that resonate with the power of the human spirit. This chapter delves into case studies unique to France, showcasing how individuals have turned adversity into avenues of learning and personal triumph. These stories are not just about overcoming challenges; they are about the transformative power of embracing them.

One such story is of Margot, a chef from Lyon, the gastronomic heart of France. Her journey began with the loss of her family's restaurant in a devastating fire. This restaurant was not just a business; it was a legacy, a piece of her heritage. The loss was profound, but Margot's response to this tragedy was remarkable. She used this adversity as a catalyst for growth. Traveling across France, she learned diverse culinary skills, eventually opening a new restaurant that fused traditional and modern cooking. Margot's story is a testament to the power of resilience and the beauty of blending old with new, creating something uniquely beautiful in the process.

Another inspiring case is of Jean-Luc, a vineyard owner in Bordeaux. A severe storm destroyed much of his crop, a disaster for any winemaker. However, Jean-Luc saw this as an opportunity to innovate. He began experimenting with new grape varieties and sustainable farming techniques. His vineyard not only recovered but also became a leader in ecological wine production. Jean-Luc's journey highlights how adversity can be a gateway to innovation and environmental stewardship.

These stories from France illustrate a universal truth: adversity is an integral part of the human experience, but it does not have to define us. Instead, it can be a driving force for learning, growth, and transformation.

The key to turning adversity into opportunity lies in our perspective. It's about making the decision to see challenges not as insurmountable obstacles but as stepping stones. Small changes in our approach and mindset can lead to significant life transformations. It's about embracing the moment, understanding that within every challenge lies the seed of an equal or greater benefit.

Another crucial aspect is the willingness to learn and adapt. In both Margot and Jean-Luc's stories, their success came from their openness to new experiences and their adaptability. They were not afraid to step out of their comfort zones, to try new things, and to learn from their experiences.

The case studies from France offer valuable insights into the art of turning adversity into growth. They remind us that our response to challenges can shape our destinies. As you navigate through your own life's challenges, remember these stories of resilience and transformation. Embrace your adversities, learn from them, and let them propel you towards your own unique path of growth and success.

Remember, in the rich tapestry of life, every thread of challenge is intertwined with potential and opportunity for personal empowerment and triumph.

The Unyielding Spirit: Resilience as the Key to Overcoming Challenges

In the dynamic and often unpredictable journey of life, resilience stands as a beacon of hope, a powerful force that enables us to overcome challenges and emerge stronger. This chapter is dedicated to unraveling the role of resilience, not just as a trait but as a crucial skill in navigating life's storms. It's about understanding how resilience can be cultivated, honed, and utilized to transform challenges into opportunities for growth and empowerment.

Resilience is often misconstrued as an inherent quality, something you either have or you don't. But the truth is far more empowering: resilience is a skill that can be developed, a muscle that can be strengthened over time. It's about the ability to bounce back from setbacks, to adapt in the face of adversity, and to keep moving forward even when the odds seem stacked against you.

Consider the story of Lucas, a young entrepreneur whose startup faced near-collapse during an economic downturn. For Lucas, this challenge was a defining moment. Instead of succumbing to despair, he chose to view this crisis as a learning opportunity. He reevaluated his business model, sought advice, and made tough decisions to pivot his strategy. This resilience not only saved his business but also propelled it to new heights. Lucas's story is a testament to the power of resilience in turning adversity into triumph.

The heart of resilience lies in how we respond to challenges. It's in the small, everyday choices we make when faced with obstacles. Do we give up, or do we look for solutions? Do we dwell on the problem, or do we focus on what can be learned from the situation? These decisions, though they may seem insignificant at the moment, shape the trajectory of our lives.

One key aspect of building resilience is maintaining a positive, yet realistic outlook. It's about embracing optimism, not as wishful thinking, but as a tool for problem-solving. A positive mindset helps us to see beyond the immediate hurdle and identify potential paths forward.

Another crucial element is the support system. Resilient individuals often have strong networks of friends, family, or mentors who provide support, advice, and perspective. These relationships are vital, offering a foundation of stability and encouragement when challenges arise.

Resilience also involves self-awareness and emotional regulation. It's about understanding your emotions, recognizing your stress triggers, and developing strategies to manage them effectively. Practices like mindfulness, meditation, and reflective journaling can be incredibly helpful in cultivating this aspect of resilience.

The role of resilience in overcoming challenges cannot be overstated. It's a dynamic and multifaceted skill that empowers us to face adversity head-on, to learn from it, and to grow through it. As you navigate your own life's challenges, remember the power of resilience. Embrace it as a tool for transformation and empowerment. Remember, each challenge you face is an opportunity to strengthen your resilience muscle, to write your story of triumph and perseverance. In the narrative of your life, let resilience be the theme that weaves through every challenge, turning each setback into a step forward on your path to success and fulfillment.

Alchemy of the Soul: Transforming Pain into Wisdom

Painful experiences are often the dark threads that seem to overshadow the brighter hues. However, these experiences hold a hidden power - the power to transform pain into wisdom. This chapter delves into practical techniques for making this transformative journey, turning our deepest struggles into profound life lessons. It's about embracing the challenges we face, not as burdens, but as opportunities to grow, learn, and empower ourselves.

The first step in this alchemy is acceptance. Acceptance does not mean resignation or defeat; it means acknowledging the reality of our pain without judgment. It's about giving ourselves permission to feel our emotions fully, whether it's sadness, anger, or fear. This acceptance is crucial because healing and wisdom can only begin when we face our pain head-on, not when we hide from it.

Once we've accepted our pain, the next step is to seek understanding. Ask yourself, "What can I learn from this experience?" This question shifts our perspective from victimhood to agency. It turns our focus inward, prompting us to reflect on our responses, our strengths, and our vulnerabilities.

Let's consider the story of Claire, who went through a difficult divorce. The experience was painful, but it also led her to a journey of self-discovery. She learned about her capacity for resilience, her needs in a relationship, and her ability to rebuild her life independently. Claire's story exemplifies how, even in our darkest moments, there are valuable lessons to be learned.

Another powerful technique is to share your story. Sharing not only helps in processing your pain but also in transforming it into wisdom. It can be through writing, art, or speaking. When you articulate your experience, you not only help yourself but also offer guidance and support to others who might be facing similar challenges.

It's also essential to practice self-compassion. Often, we are our harshest critics, especially when dealing with pain. Treat yourself with kindness, understanding, and patience. Remember, growth is a journey, not a destination.

Additionally, seeking support is crucial. This can be in the form of therapy, support groups, or trusted friends and family. External perspectives can provide insights that we might miss and offer the emotional support we need to navigate through our pain.

Lastly, apply your lessons. Wisdom is not just about understanding; it's about application. Take the insights you've gained and use them to make changes in your life. It could be setting healthier boundaries, pursuing new interests, or changing the way you interact with others.

Turning painful experiences into wisdom is a profound process of self-transformation. It requires courage, reflection, and a willingness to grow. As you navigate through your own painful experiences, remember that within every challenge lies a seed of wisdom waiting to be discovered. Embrace your journey with an open heart, and let your pain be the crucible in which your wisdom is forged. In the story of your life, let these experiences be the chapters where you emerge not just as a survivor, but as a sage, enriched and empowered by your trials.

From Victim to Victor: Cultivating a Mindset of Empowerment

The narrative of our lives is greatly influenced by the mindset we adopt. Shifting from a victim mentality to that of a victor is not just a change in perspective; it's a transformative process that empowers us to take control of our narrative. This chapter is dedicated to encouraging that crucial mindset shift, guiding you from a place of perceived helplessness to one of strength and proactive living. It's about redefining your story, not by changing the events of your past, but by altering your interpretation and response to them.

A victim mindset is characterized by a focus on the obstacles and injustices that one has faced. It's a passive state, where life is something that happens to you, not something you actively shape. This mindset can be all-consuming, trapping you in a cycle of negativity and helplessness. But here's the empowering truth: you have the choice and the power to change this narrative.

The first step in shifting to a victor mindset is recognizing that you have agency in your life. You are not just a bystander; you are the main player in your life story. This realization is pivotal. It moves you from a reactive stance to a proactive one, where you see yourself as capable of influencing the outcome of your life.

Consider the story of Leo, who lost his job unexpectedly. Initially, he was engulfed in feelings of injustice and fear. However, he soon realized that dwelling on these feelings wouldn't change his situation. So, he shifted his focus, viewing this setback as an opportunity to pursue a career he was truly passionate about. This mindset shift was the catalyst for Leo to start his own business, something he had always dreamed of but never pursued. Leo's story illustrates the power of transforming a challenging situation into a launching pad for personal success.

Another critical aspect of this mindset shift is changing how you frame your experiences. Instead of viewing challenges as barriers, see them as opportunities for growth and learning. This reframing is not about denying the difficulty of your experiences but about finding value and strength in them.

Resilience plays a key role in this transition. Building resilience involves developing coping strategies, nurturing a strong support network, and practicing self-care. It's about bouncing back from setbacks with a renewed sense of determination.

Practicing gratitude is another powerful tool in fostering a victor mindset. Gratitude shifts your focus from what's missing or wrong in your life to what's present and right. It's a reminder of your strengths, your achievements, and the positive aspects of your life.

Finally, take action. A victor mindset is not just about thinking differently; it's about acting differently. Set goals, make plans, and take steps, however small, towards achieving them. Each action you take reinforces your role as the creator of your life story.

In conclusion, shifting from a victim to a victor mindset is a journey of empowerment. It's about taking ownership of your life, reframing your challenges as opportunities, and actively working towards your goals. Remember, in the narrative of your life, you have the power to be the hero of your story. Embrace this journey with courage and conviction, and watch as your life transforms into a testament to your strength, resilience, and unwavering spirit of triumph.

Life's Classroom: Practical Exercises for Gleaning Wisdom from the Past

Our past experiences, both the triumphs and tribulations, are like pages in a textbook of life, rich with lessons and insights. However, extracting these lessons requires more than mere reflection; it necessitates a set of practical exercises designed to delve into these experiences and uncover the wisdom they hold. This chapter is dedicated to providing you with actionable strategies to learn from your past, turning each experience into a stepping stone towards personal growth and empowerment.

1. Reflective Journaling:

Begin with reflective journaling, a powerful tool for self-discovery. Dedicate time each day to write about your past experiences, focusing not just on what happened, but how you felt, how you reacted, and what outcomes ensued. Ask yourself questions like, "What could I have done differently?" or "What did this experience teach me about myself, others, or life in general?" This process of writing and reflecting helps in processing your emotions and drawing out key learnings.

2. The Perspective Shift:

Another valuable exercise is the perspective shift. For each significant past event, try to view it from different perspectives. How would someone else have perceived it?

What would you say to a friend who had gone through the same experience? This exercise fosters empathy and broadens your understanding, allowing you to see beyond your immediate emotions and reactions.

3. The Learning List:

Create a 'Learning List.' For each major event or phase in your life, list down what it taught you. These could be skills, personal insights, or general life lessons. This exercise not only helps in recognizing the positive takeaways from each experience but also serves as a reminder of how far you've come and how much you've grown.

4. Role Reversal:

Engage in a role reversal exercise. Imagine yourself in the shoes of the other people involved in your past experiences. What motivations might they have had? What challenges were they facing? This exercise can help in understanding the dynamics of past events and can foster forgiveness and empathy, both towards others and yourself.

5. Future Mapping:

Future mapping is another effective tool. Use your past experiences to map out your future. What do these experiences tell you about what you want or don't want in life? How can they shape your future decisions? This exercise helps in applying the lessons learned to your future choices, ensuring that your past experiences contribute to a brighter, more informed future.

6. Gratitude Practice:

Finally, incorporate a gratitude practice into your routine. Reflect on the past and identify moments, even in difficult experiences, for which you can be grateful. This could be the strength you found, the support you received, or the new paths that opened up. Gratitude shifts your focus from loss and regret to appreciation and growth.

In conclusion, these practical exercises are designed to help you extract valuable lessons from your past experiences. They are tools that empower you to learn, grow, and make more informed decisions in the future. Remember, every experience, no matter how challenging, holds a lesson. It's up to you to find it, learn from it, and use it to fuel your journey of personal empowerment and resilience. In the story of your life, let your past be a guide, not a weight, paving the way to a future filled with wisdom, growth, and fulfillment.

Chapter 5

Unique Challenges, Universal Choices - Embracing Life's Diverse Trials

Each individual faces a unique set of challenges. These challenges, as varied as the lives they touch, shape our narratives in profound ways. Yet, amidst this diversity, there exists a common thread - the universal power of choice. "Unique Challenges, Universal Choices" delves into how, regardless of the nature of our trials, the choices we make in response to them unite us in our quest for resilience, growth, and fulfillment.

Every person's life story is marked by a series of challenges, as varied as they are personal. For some, it might be overcoming financial hardship; for others, it may be battling health issues or navigating the complexities of interpersonal relationships. These challenges are as diverse as the human condition itself, each with its own nuances and complexities.

However, the diversity of these challenges does not imply a disparity in their significance. Each challenge, no matter how big or small it may seem in the eyes of the world, holds profound meaning for the individual experiencing it. It's crucial to acknowledge and respect the diversity of these experiences, understanding that what may be a minor hurdle for one can be a mountain for another.

Yet, in the midst of this diversity, a unifying element emerges - the power of choice. Every challenge presents us with a choice: to succumb or to overcome, to remain stagnant or to grow. These choices are the crucibles in which our character and destiny are forged. They are what make the human experience universally relatable, regardless of the varied backdrops against which our individual stories unfold.

Let's consider the story of Elena, a single mother balancing a career while raising her children. Her challenges are multifaceted, encompassing financial strain, time management, and the emotional demands of parenthood. Yet, in each of these challenges, Elena faces a choice. She chooses to view each day as an opportunity, each obstacle as a chance to teach her children resilience and optimism.

Another example is Raj, who immigrated to a new country, grappling with cultural differences and identity struggles. His journey is one of adaptation and self-discovery. Each day, he makes the choice to embrace his new environment while honoring his cultural heritage, finding strength in his diverse experiences.

These stories illustrate that while our challenges are diverse, the choices we make in response to them are universal. It's about choosing hope over despair, action over inaction, and growth over stagnation.

"Unique Challenges, Universal Choices" is an ode to the diversity of life's trials and the unifying power of our responses to them. It's a reminder that while our challenges may be unique, our capacity for resilience, growth, and empowerment is universal. As you navigate your own set of challenges, remember that the choices you make in response to them are what define your journey. Embrace these choices with courage and optimism, and let them guide you towards a life of fulfillment and purpose. In the end, it's not just the challenges we face but the choices we make in their wake that weave the extraordinary narrative of our lives.

The Choice Factor: Navigating Adversity with Decision and Determination

Adversity is an inevitable path we all traverse. Yet, within these challenges lies a profound commonality – the thread of choice. This chapter, "The Choice Factor," delves into how our responses to adversity, shaped by the decisions we make, pave the way for growth, resilience, and empowerment. It's a testament to the power of choice in transforming life's toughest challenges into opportunities for profound personal development.

At the heart of every adversity lies a critical moment – a point where we stand at the crossroads of decision. It's in these moments that our true power emerges – the power to choose our response. This choice is what differentiates those who succumb to their circumstances from those who rise above them.

Take, for example, the story of Michael, a young entrepreneur whose first business venture failed spectacularly. Faced with mounting debts and a bruised ego, he was at a pivotal point. Michael could choose to view this failure as a defining limit or as a learning opportunity. He chose the latter, using the experience to build a more resilient mindset and a stronger business plan. Today, his second venture is thriving, a testament to the power of a positive, proactive choice in the face of adversity.

The common thread of choice in response to adversity is not just about making grand gestures or drastic changes. Often, it's the small, everyday decisions that accumulate to create significant life shifts. It's about choosing to see the silver lining in every dark cloud, choosing to take one more step when everything in you wants to give up, and choosing to see setbacks as setups for comebacks.

Another key aspect of harnessing the power of choice is self-awareness. Understanding your patterns, your triggers, and your usual responses to adversity is crucial. This awareness creates a space between the challenge and your response, giving you the time and clarity to make a conscious choice rather than an automatic reaction.

Practicing mindfulness is a practical way to cultivate this self-awareness. It helps in grounding your thoughts and emotions, allowing you to approach your challenges with a clear, calm mind. Mindfulness fosters a mindset that views obstacles as opportunities to learn and grow.

Remember, exercising the power of choice does not mean you will not face difficulties or that you will always make the right decision. It means you recognize that within every challenge lies the potential for growth, and you have the autonomy to direct that growth.

The common thread of choice in response to adversity is a powerful concept. It empowers us to take control of our narrative, to steer our ship even in the stormiest of seas. As you navigate your own adversities, remember that it is your choices, more than your circumstances, that define your journey. Embrace this power of choice, and let it guide you to a path of resilience, strength, and personal empowerment. In the story of your life, let your choices be the ink with which you write your most compelling chapters.

Striking the Balance: Acceptance and Change in Personal Challenges

Balancing acceptance and change is akin to walking a tightrope. It requires skill, focus, and an understanding that both elements are crucial in navigating life's challenges. This chapter, "Striking the Balance," explores the delicate interplay between accepting what is and the drive to change what can be. It's about harnessing the power of both acceptance and change to create a life that resonates with strength, resilience, and fulfillment.

Acceptance is often the first step in facing any personal challenge. It involves acknowledging the reality of the situation without resistance or denial. This acceptance does not equate to passivity or resignation; rather, it's a recognition of the present moment as it is. It's about understanding that some aspects of life are beyond our control and that sometimes, the only thing we can change is our perspective.

Let's consider the story of Anna, who was diagnosed with a chronic illness. Initially, she struggled with denial and anger, unable to accept her new limitations. But with time, Anna realized that acceptance was not surrender; it was the starting point of her journey. She learned to embrace her new reality, finding ways to live a full and meaningful life within the bounds of her condition. This acceptance was empowering; it freed her from the shackles of "what ifs" and enabled her to focus on "what now."

However, acceptance is just one side of the coin. The other side is change – the drive to improve, to grow, and to alter our circumstances where possible. Change is about taking proactive steps, making decisions that steer our life in the direction we desire. It's about recognizing that while we can't control everything, we have the power to control our actions, reactions, and decisions.

Change is exemplified in the story of David, who found himself in a career that no longer fulfilled him. While he accepted his current skill set and experience, he also recognized his power to change his situation. David embarked on a journey of learning and self-improvement, acquiring new skills that eventually led him to a more fulfilling career path. His story illustrates that acceptance of the current state does not prevent us from working towards a different future.

Balancing acceptance and change involves a deep understanding of what can and cannot be altered. It requires the wisdom to recognize the difference and the courage to act accordingly. It's about asking ourselves the tough questions: "Can I change this situation, or do I need to change my approach to it?"

The balance between acceptance and change is a dynamic and ongoing process. It's a dance between embracing what is and creating what can be. As you navigate your personal challenges, remember to find your balance. Accept with grace what you cannot change, and pursue with determination what you can. This balance is the key to not just surviving life's challenges, but thriving through them. In the intricate story of your life, let acceptance and change be the two wings that enable you to soar.

Choosing Power: Strategies for Empowered Decision-Making

At the core of personal empowerment lies our ability to make choices - choices that steer our lives in directions we aspire to reach. This chapter, "Choosing Power," focuses on strategies that can transform your decision-making process into an empowering journey. It's about equipping you with the tools to make choices that align with your values, goals, and the life you envision for yourself. It's not just about making decisions; it's about making decisions that empower you.

1. Align Choices with Values and Goals:

The first strategy is to align your choices with your core values and long-term goals. Every decision, no matter how small, is a step towards or away from the future you desire. Begin by defining your values and what you ultimately want to achieve. When faced with a choice, ask yourself, "Does this align with my values? Will this move me closer to my goals?" This approach ensures that your decisions are purposeful and contribute to a coherent life trajectory.

2. Gather Information and Weigh Options:

Empowered decision-making involves informed decision-making. Gather as much information as possible about your options. This might involve researching, seeking advice, or considering past experiences. Weigh the pros and cons of each option, considering both short-term and long-term implications. This doesn't mean you should get stuck in analysis paralysis, but rather that you should be as informed as possible when making your choice.

3. Trust Your Instincts:

While logical analysis is important, don't underestimate the power of your instincts. Often, your gut feeling is a culmination of your subconscious knowledge and experiences. If something feels off, it's worth taking a moment to consider why. Trusting your instincts can be particularly powerful in personal or value-driven decisions.

4. Embrace the Learning Curve:

Not every decision will lead to the desired outcome, and that's okay. Viewing choices as learning opportunities rather than just success or failure is empowering. If a decision doesn't yield the expected results, take it as a chance to learn and grow. Ask yourself, "What can I take away from this experience? How can it inform my future decisions?"

5. Overcome Fear of Making Mistakes:

Fear of making the wrong choice can be paralyzing. Overcoming this fear is a crucial part of empowered decision-making. Remember, mistakes are part of the learning process. They are not reflections of your worth or ability. Embrace the possibility of failure as a natural part of growth and change.

6. Practice Decisiveness:

Finally, practice being decisive. Start with small decisions, like choosing a meal or planning your day, and work your way up to bigger ones. The more you practice, the more confident and empowered you will become in your decision-making abilities.

Empowered decision-making is a skill that can be honed through practice, reflection, and a clear understanding of your values and goals. By adopting these strategies, you can transform your decision-making process from one of uncertainty and apprehension to one of power and purpose. Remember, each choice you make is a brick in the foundation of your life. Choose wisely, choose boldly, and build the life you've always envisioned.

The Light of Choice: French Tales of Positivity and Perseverance

Amidst the rich tapestry of French culture, history, and landscapes, there are countless stories of individuals who chose positivity in the face of adversity. These narratives are not just about facing challenges; they're about transforming them through the power of choice, optimism, and resilience. This chapter, "The Light of Choice," celebrates the spirit of those who, amidst the trials of life, chose to embrace positivity, demonstrating the profound impact of attitude and decision-making on the trajectory of one's life.

In the picturesque region of Provence, there's the story of Claudette, a vineyard owner. A few years back, her vineyard was hit by an unforeseen pestilence, threatening the very heart of her family's legacy. Faced with this adversity, Claudette had two choices: succumb to despair or seek solutions with hope. She chose the latter. With unwavering positivity, she researched eco-friendly methods to rejuvenate her vineyard, eventually turning it into a model of sustainable viticulture. Claudette's story is a testament to how a positive outlook can not only overcome adversity but also pave the way for innovative solutions.

Another inspiring tale comes from the bustling streets of Paris, where we meet Marc, a young graphic designer. Marc's life took an unexpected turn when an accident left him with a physical disability. While the road to recovery was fraught with challenges, Marc's choice to remain positive and focus on his abilities, rather than his limitations, was transformative. He adapted his work methods and continued to pursue his passion for art, eventually holding an exhibition that celebrated the beauty of resilience. Marc's story illustrates that positivity is a choice that can lead to new, sometimes even more fulfilling paths.

These stories from France emphasize a powerful message: the circumstances we face may not always be within our control, but our response to them is. Choosing positivity in the face of adversity is a decision that can dramatically alter our experiences, turning obstacles into opportunities for growth and learning.

The power of small changes, a consistent theme in these narratives, is especially poignant. Small acts of optimism, incremental steps towards a solution, and the daily choice to focus on the positive aspects can accumulate into significant life transformations. It's about finding joy in the little things, maintaining hope during tough times, and believing in the possibility of a brighter tomorrow.

"The Light of Choice" is a celebration of the human spirit's capacity to choose positivity in the midst of life's challenges. The stories of Claudette, Marc, and many others across France serve as powerful reminders of the strength we possess to shape our lives through our attitudes and choices. As you navigate your own adversities, remember these tales of resilience and optimism. Let them inspire you to choose positivity, to make small yet impactful changes, and to embrace the empowering belief that, in the end, the light of hope and positivity can guide you through even the darkest of times.

Reflective Pathways: A Guide to Evaluating Your Life Choices

Navigating life's myriad choices can be akin to walking through a labyrinth; it requires careful thought, reflection, and a clear sense of direction. "Reflective Pathways" is a chapter dedicated to guiding you through a process of introspection, helping you evaluate the choices you've made and their impact on your life's trajectory. This journey of reflection is not just about looking back; it's about gleaning insights that can inform your future decisions, steering you towards a life of empowerment and fulfillment.

1. The Mirror of Past Decisions:

Start by looking back at some of the significant decisions you've made in your life. Reflect on why you made these choices. What were your motivations? Were they driven by your values, desires, fears, or external pressures? Understanding the 'why' behind your choices is crucial in learning from them.

2. The Ripple Effect:

Consider the outcomes of these decisions. How have they shaped your life? Think about both the immediate and long-term effects. This reflection can help you understand the ripple effect of your choices, illuminating how even seemingly small decisions can have significant impacts.

3. The Alignment Check:

Now, assess how these choices align with your core values and long-term goals. Have your decisions brought you closer to the life you want to live, or have they diverted you from your path? This alignment check is a powerful tool for ensuring that your future choices are more closely aligned with your true aspirations.

4. The Lessons Learned:

Every choice, whether it leads to success or setbacks, carries valuable lessons. Reflect on what you've learned from both your triumphs and your mistakes. What wisdom can you carry forward? How can these lessons shape your future decision-making?

5. The Path Forward:

Finally, based on these reflections, think about the changes you might want to make in your approach to decision-making. Identify areas where you can be more deliberate, more aligned with your values, and more cognizant of the potential impacts of your choices.

To make these reflections more concrete, consider writing them down in a journal. This act of writing not only helps in processing your thoughts but also serves as a tangible record of your growth and evolution over time.

"Reflective Pathways" is about taking the time to pause and look inward, to understand the motives, outcomes, and lessons of our past choices. It's about using these insights to make more empowered and intentional decisions in the future. Remember, each choice you make is a thread in the tapestry of your life. By reflecting on these choices and learning from them, you can weave a tapestry that reflects the true essence of who you are and the life you aspire to lead. Embrace this journey of reflection with an open heart and mind, and let it guide you towards a future brimming with purpose, fulfillment, and empowerment.

Chapter 6

Shattering Perfection - Embracing Life's Imperfections

In a world that often idolizes the idea of a 'perfect' life or circumstance, it's easy to fall into the trap of waiting for ideal situations before taking action. "Shattering Perfection" aims to dismantle this notion, challenging the idea that the perfect time, condition, or opportunity is necessary to achieve success and happiness. This chapter is about embracing life's imperfections, understanding that the pursuit of an ideal situation is often a barrier to living a fulfilling and empowered life.

The myth of ideal situations can manifest in many ways. Waiting for the perfect time to start a new venture, the perfect condition to pursue a dream, or the perfect opportunity to make a change - these are all scenarios where the myth takes root. However, the truth is, life is inherently unpredictable and seldom offers perfect conditions. The pursuit of perfection often leads to inaction, procrastination, and missed opportunities.

Let's consider the story of Laura, a writer who always dreamt of writing a novel. She kept waiting for the perfect time - when her job would be less demanding, her personal life more stable, and her finances more secure. However, that perfect time never came. It was only when Laura embraced the imperfection of her situation and started writing in the midst of her busy life that her dream began to take shape. Her novel, written in the early mornings and late nights of her 'imperfect' life, eventually became a bestseller.

Another aspect of this myth is the illusion of perfect people or relationships. The idea that there is a perfect partner, friend, or mentor out there can lead to unrealistic expectations and dissatisfaction. Real relationships are built on understanding, compromise, and growth, not perfection.

To challenge the notion of ideal situations, start by acknowledging and accepting life's imperfections. Recognize that waiting for perfection is often an excuse rooted in fear of failure or uncertainty. Embracing the imperfections in timing, circumstances, and people can be liberating and can spur you into action.

A practical step in this process is to identify areas in your life where you're waiting for perfection. Ask yourself, "What am I putting off in search of the ideal situation?" Then, challenge yourself to take a step, however small, towards your goal in your current, less-than-perfect circumstances.

It's also important to celebrate progress, not just perfection. Focus on the journey, the learning, and the growth, rather than just the outcome. Every step forward, no matter how small, is a victory in itself.

"Shattering Perfection" is an invitation to embrace life's imperfections and to understand that the perfect situation is a myth. It's a call to action, encouraging you to start where you are, use what you have, and do what you can. Remember, it's in the real, messy, and imperfect journey of life that the most beautiful stories are written. Let go of the illusion of perfection, and embrace the beauty and empowerment of living a real and meaningful life.

The Mirage of Perfection: Understanding the Drawbacks of Chasing Ideal Situations

In our pursuit of success and happiness, we often find ourselves chasing ideal situations – those perfect moments we believe are necessary for taking action or making a change. However, this quest for the perfect scenario is akin to chasing a mirage. "The Mirage of Perfection" aims to analyze the drawbacks of this pursuit, highlighting how it can hinder personal growth, delay action, and skew our perception of reality. This chapter is about recognizing the pitfalls of seeking perfection and embracing the power of progress in the present, imperfect conditions.

The Illusion of the Right Time:

One of the most significant drawbacks of chasing ideal situations is the illusion of the 'right time.' We often wait for the perfect timing to pursue our goals, but this waiting can turn into a perpetual delay. Life's unpredictability means that the perfect time rarely arrives. This pursuit of the right time can lead to missed opportunities and regrets. The key is to recognize that the best time to start is often now, with whatever resources and circumstances you have at hand.

Paralysis by Analysis:

Another challenge is paralysis by analysis. In the quest for the perfect situation, we can become over-analytical, overthinking every possible scenario. This over-analysis can lead to indecision and inaction. It's important to strike a balance between thoughtful planning and decisive action. Sometimes, taking a leap, even with some uncertainty, can be more beneficial than prolonged contemplation.

Unrealistic Expectations:

Chasing ideal situations often leads to setting unrealistic expectations. This pursuit can distort our perception of what is achievable and sustainable. When these unrealistic standards are not met, it can lead to feelings of inadequacy and disappointment. Embracing a more realistic approach helps in setting achievable goals, leading to a more satisfying and successful journey.

Diminished Appreciation for the Present:

This relentless pursuit can also diminish our appreciation for the present. Constantly looking for perfect circumstances can make us overlook the value and opportunities available in our current situation. Learning to appreciate and utilize what we currently have is crucial for personal growth and happiness.

The Pressure of Perfectionism:

The chase for ideal situations is often fueled by perfectionism. While striving for excellence is commendable, perfectionism can create unnecessary pressure and stress. It can also stifle creativity and risk-taking, essential components of innovation and personal development.

Embracing Imperfection and Action:

Instead of chasing perfect situations, embracing imperfection and taking action is more empowering. It involves understanding that growth happens in the process, not just the outcome. It's about learning from the journey, adapting to challenges, and making the most of what you have at the moment.

"The Mirage of Perfection" encourages a shift in perspective – from seeking ideal situations to making the best of the present. It's about understanding that perfection is an illusion and that true progress lies in taking action, embracing imperfections, and learning from every step of the journey. Remember, in the beautiful messiness of life, the most profound growth and accomplishments often occur. Let go of the pursuit of perfection and embrace the empowering journey of growth in the here and now.

Embracing Change: The Vital Role of Adaptability and Resilience

Adaptability and resilience stand as crucial pillars supporting our ability to navigate the unpredictable tides of change. This chapter, "Embracing Change," delves into the importance of these key attributes, highlighting how they empower us to face life's uncertainties with strength and confidence. It's about understanding that the ability to adapt and bounce back from adversity is not just a survival mechanism, but a pathway to personal growth and fulfillment.

Adaptability: The Art of Navigating Change:

Adaptability is the skill of being flexible and responsive to changing circumstances. It involves an openness to new experiences and the willingness to modify your thoughts, behaviors, and strategies in response to new information. In a world that is constantly changing, adaptability is no longer a luxury; it's a necessity.

Consider the story of Sofia, a teacher who had to suddenly shift to online teaching due to a global crisis. Initially overwhelmed by the new technology and teaching methods, Sofia embraced the change. She took courses, sought advice from colleagues, and experimented with different online tools. Her willingness to adapt not only made her an effective online educator but also opened up new opportunities for professional growth.

Resilience: The Power to Overcome and Thrive:

Resilience is the ability to withstand and bounce back from challenges and adversities. It's about facing setbacks with determination and seeing them as temporary and surmountable. Resilience doesn't mean you don't experience stress, pain, or difficulty; it means you have developed the tools to deal with them effectively.

For instance, take the story of Amir, who experienced a significant career setback when his company downsized. Despite the initial shock and uncertainty, Amir's resilience propelled him forward. He used this time to reevaluate his career goals, upgrade his skills, and eventually found a job that was more aligned with his passions. His resilience turned a challenging situation into a catalyst for positive change.

Cultivating Adaptability and Resilience:

To cultivate adaptability, start by embracing a growth mindset. See change as an opportunity to learn and grow. Be curious, ask questions, and be willing to step out of your comfort zone. Experiment with new approaches and be open to altering your path based on what you learn.

Building resilience involves fostering a positive outlook, maintaining strong relationships, and developing coping strategies. It's about taking care of your mental and physical health, setting realistic expectations, and practicing self-compassion. Remember, resilience is not inherent; it's built through experiences and conscious effort.

The Interplay of Adaptability and Resilience:

Adaptability and resilience often work hand in hand. Being adaptable allows you to navigate through changes more easily, reducing stress and anxiety. At the same time, being resilient helps you to recover from the challenges that come with change, enabling you to adapt more effectively.

"Embracing Change" highlights the indispensable roles of adaptability and resilience in our lives. In a world that is constantly in flux, these skills are essential for not just surviving but thriving. As you face the ups and downs of life, remember that your ability to adapt and your resilience are your greatest assets. Cultivate them, cherish them, and use them to navigate the beautiful journey of life with empowerment and grace.

Flourishing Against the Odds: Triumphs in Less-Than-Ideal Conditions

Life often throws us into situations far from what we would consider ideal. Yet, it's in these less-than-perfect conditions that some of the most inspiring stories of triumph and personal growth are written. "Flourishing Against the Odds" is a tribute to real-life examples of individuals who have not just survived, but thrived in challenging environments. This chapter celebrates the resilience of the human spirit and the power of determination, underscoring the belief that our circumstances do not define us, but rather, how we respond to them does.

Consider the story of Nadia, a young entrepreneur from a small, underprivileged community. Lacking resources and support, her dream of starting a business seemed distant. Yet, Nadia turned these challenges into opportunities. She used her limited resources creatively, learned through free online courses, and gradually built a network from scratch. Her journey wasn't easy, but her determination to thrive in less-than-ideal conditions led to the successful launch of her own small business, which also uplifted her community.

Then there's the story of James, who was diagnosed with a chronic illness that drastically altered his lifestyle and career plans. Faced with physical limitations and the need to redefine his identity, James found solace and strength in writing. What started as a therapeutic exercise turned into a passion, leading to the publication of his first novel. James' story is a powerful testament to the fact that even in our darkest moments, we can find new paths that lead to fulfillment and success.

These stories highlight a crucial lesson: thriving in less-than-ideal conditions often requires a shift in perspective. It's about focusing on what can be done rather than what can't, and seeing obstacles as stepping stones rather than roadblocks.

One way to cultivate this mindset is by practicing gratitude. Focusing on what you are thankful for, even in tough times, can shift your perspective and open your eyes to opportunities you might have otherwise overlooked. It's about finding the silver lining in every cloud and using it to light your way forward.

Another key aspect is resourcefulness. When resources are scarce, creativity becomes your greatest asset. It's about making the most of what you have, finding innovative solutions, and being open to learning new skills.

Embracing adaptability is also crucial. Being flexible and willing to adjust your plans can make a significant difference in how you navigate challenging conditions. It's about being fluid in your approach and open to new methods of achieving your goals.

It serves as a reminder that while we may not always have control over our circumstances, we have control over our responses to them. Let these stories inspire you to look beyond your conditions, to harness your inner strength, and to write your own story of triumph, no matter the odds. Remember, in the garden of life, the most beautiful flowers often bloom in the unlikeliest of places.

Crafting Clarity: Developing a Realistic and Positive Outlook

The way we view the world plays a pivotal role. Developing a realistic and positive outlook is not about donning rose-colored glasses to view the world; it's about cultivating a perspective that combines optimism with pragmatism. "Crafting Clarity" delves into strategies to balance hope and reality, ensuring that your outlook empowers and propels you forward, rather than holding you back. This chapter is a guide to fostering an outlook that is both grounded in reality and infused with positivity.

Embracing the Power of Yet:

A key strategy in developing a realistic and positive outlook is embracing the power of 'yet.' This simple word transforms statements of limitation into statements of possibility. Instead of saying, "I can't do this," say, "I can't do this yet." This shift in language fosters a growth mindset, acknowledging current limitations while leaving room for improvement and learning.

Balancing Optimism with Pragmatism:

Cultivating a balanced outlook involves acknowledging the positive aspects of a situation without ignoring the challenges. It's about being optimistic about the future while also being prepared to face potential obstacles. This balance prevents the disillusionment that often comes from unbridled optimism or the paralysis that can accompany excessive pessimism.

Learning from Setbacks:

Every setback or failure is an opportunity for learning and growth. Adopt a habit of analyzing your setbacks to extract lessons from them. Ask yourself, "What can this experience teach me? How can I use this knowledge moving forward?" This approach turns challenges into valuable experiences that contribute to a positive and realistic outlook.

Practicing Gratitude:

Gratitude is a powerful tool for developing a positive outlook. Regularly take time to reflect on the things you are grateful for. This could be as simple as appreciating a sunny day, the support of a friend, or your own progress and achievements. Gratitude shifts your focus from what's lacking to what's abundant in your life.

Setting Realistic Goals:

Setting achievable, realistic goals is crucial. Unrealistic goals can lead to disappointment and a negative outlook, while achievable goals foster a sense of accomplishment and positivity. Break your larger goals into smaller, manageable steps to make them more attainable.

Mindfulness and Reflection:

Mindfulness practices, such as meditation or deep breathing exercises, help in maintaining a calm and clear mind. This clarity allows you to assess situations realistically and respond with a positive outlook. Regular reflection on your thoughts and feelings also helps in understanding your outlook and making necessary adjustments.

Seeking Diverse Perspectives:

Expose yourself to diverse perspectives and experiences. This broadens your understanding of the world and prevents a narrow or biased outlook. Engage in conversations with people who have different viewpoints, read widely, and be open to new ideas and experiences.

It's about finding that sweet spot where you can view life's challenges with a positive lens, without losing sight of reality. Embrace these strategies to cultivate an outlook that not only brightens your view of the world but also strengthens your ability to navigate it with confidence, resilience, and hope. Remember, the lens through which you view the world shapes your experience of it, so choose a lens that empowers you.

Embracing Reality: Exercises for Accepting Life As It Is

In our quest for fulfillment and happiness, we often get caught up in how we wish life would be, overlooking the beauty and opportunities of life as it is. "Embracing Reality" offers practical exercises designed to ground you in the present and help you appreciate the value of your current circumstances. This chapter is about shifting focus from an idealized version of life to embracing the real, tangible moments that constitute our daily existence. It's a journey towards empowerment and resilience, rooted in the acceptance and appreciation of life in its true form.

1. Mindfulness Meditation:

Start with mindfulness meditation. This practice involves focusing on the present moment, observing your thoughts and feelings without judgment. Spend a few minutes each day in a quiet space, focusing on your breath and observing your thoughts as they come and go. This exercise helps you to become more aware and appreciative of the present, reducing the longing for things to be different.

2. The Gratitude Journal:

Maintain a gratitude journal. Each day, write down three things you are grateful for in your current life. These could be simple joys like a sunny day, a good meal, or a pleasant conversation. This practice shifts your focus from what's missing to what's present, fostering a sense of contentment and acceptance.

3. Reality Check Exercise:

Engage in a reality check exercise. Write down your idealized version of life on one side of a page and your current life on the other. Then, identify aspects of your current life that align with your ideal version. This exercise helps in recognizing that while life may not be perfect, it often contains elements of our ideal scenarios.

4. Mindful Observation:

Practice mindful observation. Choose an everyday activity like eating, walking, or showering. Focus entirely on the experience, engaging all your senses. Notice the sights, sounds, smells, and sensations. This practice enhances your appreciation for everyday experiences, grounding you in the reality of the present moment.

5. The 'As If' Exercise:

Try the 'as if' exercise. For a day, behave 'as if' your current life is your ideal life. Embrace each moment and find joy in the mundane. This exercise helps in shifting your perspective, showing you how much of your happiness is dependent on your outlook rather than your circumstances.

6. Letting Go Visualization:

Engage in a letting go visualization. Close your eyes and imagine letting go of your desires for an ideal life. Visualize them floating away, leaving you with a sense of peace and acceptance of your current life. This exercise can be powerful in releasing the hold of unmet desires and unrealistic expectations.

Chapter 7

Breaking Free from the Trap of Self-Victimization

In the narrative of our lives, we sometimes unknowingly cast ourselves in the role of the victim, a mindset that can be subtly debilitating. This chapter is about understanding why we fall into the pattern of self-victimization and how to empower ourselves to step out of it, embracing a mindset of resilience and agency.

Understanding the Psychology Behind Self-Victimization:

Self-victimization often stems from a complex interplay of past experiences, belief systems, and coping mechanisms. It can be rooted in past traumas, where victimization was a reality, leading to a mindset that continually perceives oneself as a victim in various life scenarios. This mindset is further fueled by a sense of powerlessness and a belief that external factors solely dictate one's life.

The Role of Learned Helplessness:

A key concept in understanding self-victimization is learned helplessness, a state where individuals believe they have no control over the outcomes in their lives, leading to passive acceptance of their circumstances. This often develops after experiencing repeated negative events that one perceives as uncontrollable.

Recognizing Self-Victimization Patterns:

The first step in overcoming self-victimization is recognizing its patterns. This involves being aware of your internal dialogue. Do you find yourself often blaming others or external circumstances for your challenges? Do you feel like things always happen to you, rather than you having a role in shaping them? Acknowledging these patterns is crucial for change.

Reframing the Narrative:

Reframing your narrative is about shifting your perspective. Instead of viewing challenges as things happening to you, see them as opportunities for growth. This shift moves you from a passive recipient of life's challenges to an active participant in shaping your journey.

Cultivating Self-Efficacy:

Building a sense of self-efficacy, or belief in your ability to influence events and outcomes in your life, is critical. Start by setting small, achievable goals and gradually work your way up. Celebrate your successes, no matter how small, as they reinforce your sense of agency.

Seeking Support and Building Resilience:

Professional support, like therapy, can be invaluable in understanding and overcoming patterns of self-victimization. Additionally, building resilience – the ability to bounce back from setbacks – is essential. Resilience can be cultivated through practices like mindfulness, stress management techniques, and developing a strong support network.

Beyond the Victim Mentality: Embracing Growth and Empowerment

The concept of a victim mentality, where one perceives themselves consistently as a victim of circumstances, can significantly influence personal growth and life trajectory. This chapter is not just about identifying the pitfalls of a victim mentality but also about outlining strategies to overcome it, fostering a mindset of resilience, responsibility, and proactive change.

Understanding the Victim Mentality:

A victim mentality often stems from past experiences where one felt powerless or mistreated. Over time, this can evolve into a habitual way of viewing the world, where one feels perpetually at the mercy of external forces. This mindset can lead to a cycle of negativity, inaction, and helplessness, impeding personal growth and the ability to cope effectively with life's challenges.

Impact on Personal Growth:

The long-term impact of a victim mentality is far-reaching. It can lead to missed opportunities, as individuals may avoid taking risks or trying new experiences due to fear of failure or further victimization. It can hinder relationships, as continual self-victimization can strain interactions with others, often leading to a lack of accountability and self-awareness. Moreover, it can stifle resilience, as viewing oneself as a perpetual victim leaves little room for developing the strength and adaptability needed to overcome life's hurdles.

Shifting the Perspective:

Moving beyond a victim mentality requires a conscious shift in perspective. It involves acknowledging past hurts without allowing them to dictate the present. This shift is about taking ownership of your life and recognizing that, while you cannot control everything that happens to you, you can control how you respond to life's events.

Strategies for Overcoming Victim Mentality:

1. Cultivate Self-Awareness: Regular self-reflection can help identify patterns of victim-like thinking. Mindfulness practices can be particularly effective in developing this awareness.

2. Practice Accountability: Taking responsibility for your actions and their outcomes is crucial. This doesn't mean blaming yourself for everything; it's about understanding your role in various aspects of your life.

3. Set Empowering Goals: Focus on setting and achieving goals that reinforce your agency. This practice can help shift your mindset from one of passivity to one of active engagement in your life.

4. Seek Support and Guidance: Sometimes, overcoming a deeply ingrained victim mentality requires professional help, such as therapy or counseling. These resources can provide valuable tools and insights.

5. Embrace Resilience: Develop resilience by challenging yourself to face and overcome small obstacles. This can gradually build your confidence in handling larger challenges.

6. Focus on Solutions: Instead of dwelling on problems or perceived injustices, direct your energy

towards finding solutions and making positive changes.

Understanding the Difference: Genuine Victimization vs. Self-Imposed Victimhood

Navigating life's complex journey often involves encountering genuine victimization as well as falling into patterns of self-imposed victimhood.

Genuine Victimization: Acknowledging Real Hurt and Injustice

Genuine victimization occurs when an individual experiences harm, injustice, or mistreatment, whether physically, emotionally, or psychologically, due to external factors beyond their control. It's important to acknowledge and validate these experiences. Victims of such circumstances often require support, understanding, and resources to heal and rebuild.

Self-Imposed Victimhood: The Role of Mindset and Perspective

In contrast, self-imposed victimhood is often a product of mindset and perspective. It arises when individuals perceive themselves as perpetual victims, regardless of their actual circumstances. This mindset is characterized by a focus on grievances, a sense of powerlessness, and a belief that external factors are solely to blame for one's misfortunes. Unlike genuine victimization, self-imposed victimhood can be altered through changes in perspective and mindset.

Personal Anecdotes: Learning from Real-Life Experiences

Consider the story of Elena, who grew up in a challenging family environment and faced genuine victimization in her early years. As an adult, Elena recognized that while her past was painful, continually viewing herself as a victim in all situations was hindering her growth. Through therapy and self-reflection, she learned to differentiate her past experiences from her current capabilities, moving towards a more empowered and proactive stance in life.

Strategies for Overcoming Self-Imposed Victimhood

1. Self-Awareness: Cultivate self-awareness to recognize patterns of self-victimization. Reflect on your thoughts and attitudes regularly and ask whether they are reflective of your current situation or rooted in past experiences.

2. Empowerment through Action: Shift from a passive to an active role in your life. Set achievable goals and take steps towards them, affirming your agency.

3. Seek Professional Help: If distinguishing between genuine victimization and self-imposed victimhood becomes overwhelming, seeking support from a therapist or counselor can be beneficial.

4. Cultivate Resilience: Develop resilience by facing and overcoming small challenges, thus building confidence in your ability to handle life's difficulties.

5. Focus on Solutions, Not Problems: Direct your energy towards finding solutions and making

positive changes, rather than dwelling on perceived injustices or hardships.

6. Practice Gratitude: Regularly acknowledge and appreciate the positive aspects of your life. This can shift focus from what is lacking to what is abundant.

Empowerment: Breaking Free from the Victim Mindset

In the journey of life, it's easy to feel overwhelmed by circumstances and to perceive ourselves as victims of fate. This mindset, though understandable, can be a significant barrier to personal growth and happiness. The key to overcoming this mindset lies not in monumental changes, but in small, decisive actions that redirect our life's trajectory.

Firstly, recognize the power of choice. Every moment presents us with choices – how to react, how to think, and how to behave. By consciously choosing responses that align with our goals and values, we take control back from the hands of fate. For instance, when faced with a challenge, instead of asking "Why me?", ask "What can I learn from this?" This simple shift in perspective can transform obstacles into opportunities for growth.

Secondly, practice gratitude. It might seem counterintuitive, especially when things aren't going our way, but gratitude is a powerful tool. Start each day by listing three things you're grateful for. They don't have to be grand; even small joys count. This habit shifts focus from what's lacking to what's abundant in our lives, fostering a mindset of resourcefulness rather than helplessness.

Additionally, surround yourself with positivity. The people around us can significantly influence our mindset. Seek out friends, mentors, and communities that uplift and inspire you. Their energy can be contagious, helping you to adopt a more proactive and positive outlook.

Personal anecdotes play a crucial role in this transformation. Consider Jane, a friend of mine, who after years of feeling stuck in a dead-end job, decided to make a change. Each morning, she devoted fifteen minutes to learning a new skill. This small action, consistently repeated, eventually led to a new career path. Jane's story exemplifies the impact of small, consistent steps towards change.

Embrace failure as a stepping stone. Every setback is an opportunity to learn and grow. Thomas Edison famously said, "I have not failed. I've just found 10,000 ways that won't work." Adopting this mindset turns failures into valuable lessons, guiding us closer to our goals.

Finally, take care of yourself. Self-care is not selfish; it's essential. Regular exercise, adequate sleep, and healthy eating habits are foundational for a strong, resilient mindset. When we feel good physically, we're better equipped to handle mental and emotional challenges.

Breaking free from the victim mindset is a journey of small, yet powerful, deliberate choices. Recognize the power of choice, practice gratitude, surround yourself with positivity, learn from personal experiences and failures, and prioritize self-care. Each of these strategies empowers us to take control of our lives, fostering resilience and a proactive approach to life's challenges. Remember, empowerment is not just about feeling strong; it's about recognizing that you always have a choice, and it's these choices that shape your life's story.

Triumph Over Self: Stories of Overcoming Self-Victimization

It's an easy spiral to fall into, where challenges become insurmountable walls rather than stepping stones. Yet, the stories of those who have overcome this mindset serve as powerful testaments to the human spirit's resilience and the transformative power of personal responsibility and action.

Consider the story of Michael, a man I met during a seminar. He had faced a series of setbacks in his career and personal life. Burdened by these challenges, Michael had slipped into a mindset where everything seemed out of his control. But one day, he made a simple, yet life-changing decision. He started journaling his thoughts and actions each day. This small step was the catalyst for a remarkable transformation. By reflecting on his daily choices, he began to see patterns in his behavior and thought processes that contributed to his sense of victimhood. Gradually, Michael started making small changes – volunteering for new projects at work, joining a local community group, and setting aside time for self-reflection. These changes, seemingly insignificant in isolation, cumulatively led to a profound shift in his life. Michael's story is a testament to the power of self-awareness and the cumulative impact of small, daily choices.

Then there's Emma, a single mother of two, who found herself constantly overwhelmed and underappreciated. Struggling to balance work and family, she felt like a victim of her circumstances. The turning point came when Emma chose to focus on what she could control – her attitude and her actions. She began waking up an hour earlier each day to dedicate time to herself, whether for exercise, reading, or simply enjoying a quiet cup of coffee. This act of self-care became her daily anchor, providing the strength and clarity to tackle the day's challenges more effectively. Emma's journey is a powerful illustration of how nurturing oneself can dramatically shift one's perspective and experience of life.

These stories highlight a fundamental truth: the power to change our lives lies within us. It's not the grand gestures, but the small, consistent steps that pave the path to transformation. It's about shifting focus from what happens to us to how we respond. It's about understanding that while we can't control every aspect of our lives, we can always control our reactions and actions.

Encouraging and empathetic, these stories serve as a reminder that you are not alone in your struggles. Like Michael, Emma, and countless others, you too have the strength to break free from the chains of self-victimization. It starts with a decision – a decision to take responsibility for your life, to focus on the present and what can be done, rather than what can't be changed.

The journey from self-victimization to empowerment is unique for each individual, but it always begins with a choice. A choice to take that first step, no matter how small. Remember, every journey of transformation begins with a single, decisive action. Your story of triumph awaits; it's time to take that first step.

Cultivating Empowerment: Practical Exercises for a Stronger You

Empowerment isn't just a feeling; it's a state of being, and like any state, it can be cultivated and strengthened through practice. The journey towards personal empowerment is paved with small, deliberate actions that gradually build your sense of control and confidence. Below are some practical exercises designed to foster empowerment, each rooted in the philosophy of taking actionable steps to transform your life.

1. The Mirror Exercise: Affirm Your Strengths Daily

Begin each day with what I call the Mirror Exercise. Stand in front of a mirror, look yourself in the eye, and affirm three of your strengths. These could be character traits, skills, or recent achievements. This exercise is a powerful way to start your day on a positive note, reinforcing self-belief and highlighting your capabilities. It's a simple but effective way to combat negative self-talk and build a more empowered self-image.

2. Decision-Making Diary: Record and Reflect

Keep a Decision-Making Diary for at least a week. In this diary, jot down every decision you make, big or small. At the end of each day, reflect on these decisions. Ask yourself, "What motivated this choice?", "How did I feel about making this decision?", and "What were the outcomes?" This exercise heightens awareness of your decision-making process, helping you to understand and improve your ability to make choices that align with your personal and professional goals.

3. The 'Can-Do' List: Small Actions, Big Impact

Create a daily 'Can-Do' List. Unlike a typical to-do list that can sometimes feel overwhelming, the 'Can-Do' List should consist of small, achievable tasks that you are confident you can complete. Each task completed will be a small victory, reinforcing your belief in your abilities. It's about celebrating the small wins, which cumulatively build a stronger sense of self-efficacy.

4. Visualization: Picture Your Empowered Self

Visualization is a powerful tool for cultivating a sense of empowerment. Dedicate a few minutes each day to visualize yourself successfully handling a challenging situation. Imagine the details vividly – how you feel, what you say, how you react. This mental rehearsal builds confidence and prepares you to handle real-life situations more effectively.

5. Gratitude Journaling: Focus on the Positive

Keep a Gratitude Journal. Each night, write down three things you are grateful for. These can be as simple as a sunny day or a good cup of coffee. This practice shifts your focus from what you lack to what you have, fostering a mindset of abundance and possibility.

6. The 'Speak Up' Challenge: Raise Your Voice

Challenge yourself to 'speak up' in situations where you usually wouldn't. It could be sharing an idea in a meeting, expressing a preference when with friends, or addressing something that bothers you. This exercise strengthens your voice and reminds you that your opinions and needs matter.

These exercises are designed to build a foundation of self-belief and proactive action. Each one is a step towards a more empowered you. Remember, empowerment is not just about feeling strong; it's about living strong. By incorporating these exercises into your daily life, you're not only cultivating empowerment, you're actively reshaping your life's narrative into one of strength, resilience, and control.

Chapter 8

Learning from the Past, Shaping the Future

The journey of personal growth is like sailing a ship; you need to know where you've been to navigate where you're going. This chapter is about the transformative power of historical reflection, a crucial tool in shaping a brighter, more intentional future. It's about understanding that our past, with its mix of triumphs and tribulations, is not just a story to be told but a lesson to be learned.

The importance of reflecting on the past cannot be overstated. It provides us with invaluable insights into our patterns, behaviors, and decisions, helping us understand the 'whys' behind our 'whats'. More importantly, it empowers us to make conscious choices moving forward. This reflection isn't about dwelling on the past but about leveraging it as a springboard for future growth.

Let's consider a personal anecdote. Sarah, a colleague of mine, found herself constantly struggling in her professional relationships. It was only when she took the time to reflect on her past interactions that she noticed a pattern of defensiveness and resistance to feedback. Armed with this awareness, Sarah began to approach feedback differently, seeing it as an opportunity for growth rather than a personal attack. This shift not only improved her professional relationships but also accelerated her career growth.

Historical reflection also helps us appreciate how far we've come. It's easy to get caught up in the pursuit of future goals and forget to acknowledge our past achievements. Regularly looking back allows us to celebrate our progress, however small, and reinforces our belief in our ability to overcome challenges.

Another key aspect is the role of historical reflection in breaking negative cycles. By understanding our past, especially the mistakes and failures, we become better equipped to avoid repeating them. Think of it as a navigational map, guiding us away from the reefs of past errors and towards clearer waters.

Now, how do we effectively reflect on our past? It starts with setting aside dedicated time for reflection – be it through journaling, meditation, or simply quiet contemplation. During this time, ask yourself questions like: "What were my biggest lessons?", "How have I grown from these experiences?", and "What would I do differently?" This practice of questioning and introspection is a powerful tool in transforming past experiences into future wisdom.

Moreover, sharing our reflections with others can further enhance this learning process. Discussing our past with trusted friends, mentors, or family members can provide new perspectives and insights, deepening our understanding and learning.

Historical reflection is not just about looking back; it's about learning from what has been to better navigate what will be. It's a crucial step in the journey of personal empowerment, enabling us to make informed, intentional decisions that shape our future. As we move forward, let's remember that our past is a treasure trove of lessons, ready to guide us towards a more empowered, purposeful future. Let's embrace these lessons and allow them to illuminate our path ahead.

Balancing Wisdom and Aspiration: Navigating Past Lessons and Future Dreams

The key to this balance lies in understanding that our past is a reservoir of lessons, not a roadblock to our future. It's essential to reflect on our past experiences, acknowledging both our triumphs and our setbacks. This reflection helps us understand the patterns in our lives, recognize our strengths, and identify areas for growth. However, it's equally important to ensure that our past does not define our future. We must view our history as a launching pad, not an anchor.

Consider the story of Anna, a friend who once felt trapped by her past mistakes. She believed her failed business venture doomed her to a life of mediocrity.

However, when she began to view her past as a learning experience rather than a life sentence, her perspective shifted. She used the lessons from her failure to build a new, successful venture. Anna's story is a testament to the power of reframing our past as a foundation for future success.

Simultaneously, it's crucial to nurture our future aspirations. Dreams give us direction, motivation, and a sense of purpose. They propel us forward, inspiring action and innovation. However, aspirations without the grounding of past lessons can lead us astray. The trick is to dream big while planning realistically, using our past experiences as a guide.

Balancing past lessons with future aspirations involves a few practical steps:

1. Reflect and Learn: Regularly take time to reflect on your past. What worked? What didn't? How have these experiences shaped you? Use these insights to inform your future decisions.

2. Set Informed Goals: When setting goals for the future, consider the lessons from your past. Use

them to set realistic, achievable goals that still stretch and challenge you.

3. Embrace Flexibility: Understand that your path may need to adjust as you move forward. Be open to learning and adapting, using both past wisdom and future possibilities to guide you.

4. Celebrate Progress: Acknowledge and celebrate the small steps you take towards your goals. Progress, no matter how small, is a step in the right direction.

5. Stay Grounded in the Present: While learning from the past and aspiring for the future, don't forget to live in the present. It's the only moment where action can be taken.

The journey of life requires a delicate balance between the wisdom of the past and the aspirations for the future. By learning from our experiences and using them to inform our dreams, we can chart a course that is both ambitious and achievable. Remember, your past has shaped you, but it does not limit you. Your future is an open field, ready for the seeds of today's actions and yesterday's wisdom. Let's embark on this journey with an open heart and a clear mind, ready to weave the beautiful tapestry of our lives.

The Power of Release: Forgiveness and Letting Go in Personal Development

In the journey of self-growth, one of the most challenging yet transformative steps we can take is to forgive and let go. This chapter explores the pivotal role of forgiveness and the act of letting go in our personal development. It's not just about others; it's about freeing ourselves, allowing us to move forward unburdened by the weights of resentment and past hurts. It's about understanding that holding onto anger and grudges is like carrying a heavy backpack on a long hike; it slows us down and exhausts us.

Forgiveness, often misunderstood, is not about condoning wrongdoings or forgetting the pain caused. It's about accepting what happened and deciding to no longer let it control your emotions and actions. This process is crucial for personal development, as it shifts the focus from past grievances to future possibilities.

Let's consider a real-life example. Emily, a friend of mine, spent years harboring anger towards a colleague who had wronged her. This resentment not only strained her professional relationship but also impacted her personal life, as she often found herself consumed by negative thoughts. It was only when Emily chose to forgive – not for the colleague's sake but for her own peace – that she experienced a profound shift. She felt lighter, more positive, and her work and personal life improved dramatically. Emily's story illustrates that forgiveness is a gift you give to yourself.

Letting go is equally important in our journey. It involves releasing not just grudges, but also outdated self-perceptions and limiting beliefs. It's about freeing ourselves from the narratives that no longer serve us. For instance, letting go of the belief that we're not good enough can open doors to new opportunities and experiences that were previously overshadowed by self-doubt.

The process of forgiveness and letting go can be challenging, but there are practical steps to facilitate this journey:

1. Acknowledge and Express Your Feelings: Recognize the hurt and anger you feel. Bottling up emotions only gives them more power.

2. Reflect on the Impact: Understand how these feelings are affecting your life. Are they holding you back from happiness and growth?

3. Make a Conscious Decision to Forgive: Decide that you want to let go of the pain for your own well-being.

4. Seek Understanding: Sometimes understanding the why behind someone's actions can aid in the process of forgiveness. Remember, understanding is not excusing.

5. Practice Empathy: Try to see things from the other person's perspective. This can sometimes ease the process of forgiveness.

6. Embrace the Lessons: Every experience, good or bad, teaches us something. Focus on what you've learned and how it has made you stronger.

7. Let Go and Move On: Actively choose to leave the past in the past and focus on the present and future.

Forgiveness and letting go are not signs of weakness; they are acts of strength and courage. They are essential steps in the journey of personal development, enabling us to grow and evolve into our best selves. As we learn to release the chains of past hurts and limiting beliefs, we open ourselves up to a world of new possibilities and peace. Remember, the act of letting go isn't just about releasing what's behind; it's about embracing what lies ahead.

Building Blocks of Growth: Utilizing Past Experiences for a Brighter Future

Every experience in our life, whether positive or challenging, lays a brick in the foundation of our personal growth. This chapter delves into strategies for leveraging past experiences as catalysts for growth and transformation. It's about understanding that our past, with all its twists and turns, is not just a memory lane but a treasure trove of lessons and insights. It's a guidebook filled with wisdom, waiting to be used in sculpting a more empowered and fulfilling future.

The first step in using past experiences for growth is embracing them, irrespective of their nature. Often, we're tempted to bury our unpleasant experiences, but even the most painful moments carry valuable lessons. Acknowledge every experience, understand its impact, and recognize the strength and resilience it has fostered in you.

Let's consider the story of David, a colleague who experienced a significant career setback. Initially, David was engulfed by feelings of failure and self-doubt. However, upon reflecting on this experience, he realized it had taught him valuable lessons about resilience, adaptability, and the importance of networking. By viewing his setback as a learning opportunity, David was able to use these insights to propel his career in a new and more fulfilling direction.

Another strategy is to actively seek the lessons in each experience. Ask yourself: What did this experience teach me? How has it shaped my perceptions or behaviors? This process of introspection can turn experiences into meaningful lessons that inform future decisions and actions.

Additionally, it's crucial to detach from past mistakes. While it's important to learn from them, dwelling on them can hinder growth. Understand that mistakes are not a reflection of your worth but stepping stones to wisdom. Practice self-compassion and remind yourself that growth is a journey, not a destination.

Sharing your experiences with others can also be a powerful tool for growth. It not only helps in gaining different perspectives but also in reinforcing the lessons learned. Whether it's through mentoring, writing, or simply conversing with friends, sharing your journey can provide clarity and further embed the lessons in your consciousness.

Moreover, setting goals based on past learnings can be highly effective. Use your experiences to identify areas where you want to grow or change. This goal-setting, informed by past lessons, ensures that your objectives are both realistic and aligned with your personal journey.

Finally, remember to celebrate the growth that has come from past experiences. Acknowledging your progress, no matter how small, reinforces a positive mindset and motivates you to continue on your path of self-improvement.

Past experiences, be they successes or challenges, are invaluable assets in our personal growth journey. By embracing and learning from these experiences, detaching from past mistakes, sharing our stories, setting informed goals, and celebrating our growth, we can use our past as a powerful tool to build a brighter, more empowered future. Remember, your past experiences are not just chapters in your life story; they are the building blocks of your personal evolution.

Unfolding Chapters: Transformative Tales of Learning from the Past

Life is an incredible journey of learning and transformation. This chapter shares inspirational stories of individuals who harnessed the power of their past experiences, transforming their lives in remarkable ways. These narratives not only inspire but also illustrate the profound impact of reflecting on, learning from, and moving beyond our past. They embody the essence of personal empowerment, showcasing how we can steer the course of our lives towards brighter horizons by learning from where we've been.

Consider the story of Laura, a woman I met at a community workshop. Years ago, Laura found herself mired in a cycle of negative relationships and self-doubt. It was her decision to confront her past head-on that marked the beginning of her transformation. She delved into her history, identifying patterns and acknowledging the impact of her upbringing on her choices. This journey of self-discovery led to significant changes in how she viewed herself and her relationships. Today, Laura is not only thriving in a healthy relationship but also mentors young adults on self-esteem and resilience. Her story is a powerful testament to the fact that understanding our past can be the key to unlocking a more fulfilling future.

Then there's the remarkable journey of Alex, once a high-flying executive whose life seemed perfect on the surface. Following a life-altering health scare, Alex took a step back to reflect on his life's priorities. This period of introspection made him realize that his relentless pursuit of professional success left him feeling unfulfilled. Armed with these insights, Alex made a courageous decision to shift his focus towards work that was more meaningful and aligned with his values. He transitioned into non-profit work, finding immense satisfaction in making a positive impact. Alex's story underscores how reflecting on our life experiences can lead to profound personal and professional transformation.

These stories highlight a fundamental truth: our past does not have to dictate our future. Instead, it can serve as a rich source of wisdom, guiding us towards better decisions and more fulfilling paths. It's about extracting the lessons hidden in our experiences and using them to shape a future that resonates with our deepest values and aspirations.

The process of learning from the past and transforming our lives is not always easy. It requires courage, honesty, and a willingness to confront uncomfortable truths. However, the rewards of such introspection are immeasurable. It leads to personal growth, greater self-awareness, and an empowered approach to life.

The stories of Laura, Alex, and many others like them, are beacons of inspiration. They remind us that no matter where we've been or what we've been through, we have the power to chart a new course for our lives. By embracing the lessons of our past, we can embark on a journey of transformation, leading to a future rich with purpose, fulfillment, and joy. Let their stories be a reminder that in the narrative of your life, you hold the pen, and every past chapter, whether joyful or challenging, is an opportunity to write a better, more empowering future.

Charting Your Course: Guided Activities to Harness Your Past for a Brighter Tomorrow

The pages of our past are filled with lessons that, if harnessed wisely, can steer us towards a more fulfilling future. This chapter offers guided activities designed to help you delve into your personal history, extract valuable insights, and apply these lessons to your life journey. By engaging in these activities, you'll not only gain a deeper understanding of your past but also learn how to use this knowledge to empower your future.

1. Mapping Your Life Story

Start by creating a timeline of your life. Include major events, turning points, successes, and challenges. This visual representation will help you see the broader narrative of your life. Look for patterns or recurring themes. Perhaps resilience shines through your toughest times, or maybe a certain type of challenge keeps reappearing. Understanding these patterns is the first step in using your past experiences as a guide for future growth.

2. Reflective Journaling

Dedicate time each week to reflective journaling. Focus on one significant past event at a time. Write about how it impacted you, what you learned, and how it shaped your beliefs and behaviors. Reflective journaling is a powerful tool for processing experiences and extracting meaningful lessons.

3. The Wisdom Interview

Identify someone in your life who has known you for a long time and who you trust. Ask them to share their perspective on your growth and life journey. Sometimes, others can provide insights into our lives that we might overlook. This exercise can offer a fresh perspective on your past experiences and how they've contributed to the person you are today.

4. Decision Analysis

Think back to a key decision you made in your past. Analyze this decision – what led you to it, how you felt making it, and its consequences. Understanding your decision-making process and its outcomes can be incredibly enlightening, helping you make more informed decisions in the future.

5. The Letter to Your Past Self

Write a letter to your younger self. Offer advice, compassion, and insights based on what you've learned since then. This exercise fosters self-compassion and helps you realize the growth and progress you've made over the years.

6. Gratitude Mapping

Create a 'gratitude map' of your past. Identify people, experiences, and challenges that you're thankful for and why. This activity shifts your perspective, allowing you to view even difficult experiences through a lens of gratitude for the lessons they've imparted.

7. Vision Boarding Your Future

Using the insights gained from the above activities, create a vision board that represents your future goals and aspirations. This board should reflect not only what you want to achieve but also incorporate the wisdom gleaned from your past experiences.

These activities are designed to turn your past into a rich resource for personal growth and future planning. By engaging with your history, acknowledging its impact, and extracting its lessons, you equip yourself with powerful tools for shaping a future that aligns with your deepest values and aspirations. Remember, your past is a treasure trove of wisdom, waiting to be unlocked and used in charting a course towards a more empowered and fulfilling life.

Chapter 9

Beyond Complaints: Embracing Responsibility

Habitual complaining stands out as a thread that, while common, can unravel our sense of empowerment and hinder personal growth. This chapter delves into the psychology behind habitual complaining, exploring its roots and impacts, and most importantly, guiding us on a path to embracing responsibility and transforming our narrative from one of victimhood to empowerment.

Habitual complaining often stems from a feeling of powerlessness. When things don't go our way, it's easier to vocalize our dissatisfaction than to confront the more challenging aspects of our circumstances. It's a defense mechanism, shielding us from the discomfort of acknowledging our role in our life's situation. However, the irony is that while complaining might provide temporary relief, it perpetuates a sense of helplessness and passivity, trapping us in a cycle of negativity.

Understanding this cycle is the first step towards breaking it. When we complain, we focus on what is wrong, often exaggerating the severity of our predicaments. This focus reinforces a negative mindset, impacting our mood, stress levels, and even our physical health. More so, it affects how others perceive and interact with us, potentially leading to strained relationships and missed opportunities.

Let's consider a real-life example: Meet John, a colleague who was known for his constant complaining. Whether it was about work, life, or even the weather, John always had something negative to say. Over time, his peers started to distance themselves, leading to a sense of isolation and further dissatisfaction in his life. It was a self-fulfilling prophecy – his complaints about life led to more experiences that fueled his complaints.

The shift for John, and for anyone caught in the complaint cycle, comes from embracing responsibility. It's about moving from a mindset of 'things happen to me' to 'I have the power to influence my life'. This doesn't mean you have the power to control everything that happens, but you do control how you respond to what happens.

Here are actionable steps to shift from habitual complaining to empowering responsibility:

1. Awareness and Acknowledgment: The first step is to become aware of your complaining patterns. Acknowledge that while it's a natural response, it's not a productive one.

2. Seek Solutions, Not Sympathy: When tempted to complain, ask yourself, "What can I do about this?" Focusing on solutions rather than problems shifts your mindset from passive to proactive.

3. Practice Gratitude: Actively look for things in your life to be grateful for. Gratitude is a powerful antidote to complaining, as it shifts your focus from what's missing to what's present.

4. Cultivate Positive Relationships: Surround yourself with people who embody the positive, proactive attitude you aspire to. Their influence can be motivational.

5. Set Realistic Expectations: Sometimes, our complaints stem from unrealistic expectations. Adjusting these to align more closely with reality can reduce frustration.

Embracing responsibility and moving beyond habitual complaining is about changing how we interact with our world. It's a shift from a reactive stance to an empowered, proactive approach. By taking these steps, we can transform our narrative, building a life marked not by what happens to us, but by how we respond and grow from our experiences. Remember, every complaint is an opportunity to take responsibility, find solutions, and move closer to the life we aspire to live.

The Downward Spiral of Constant Complaining

In the journey of life, our words and thoughts shape our reality. Constant complaining, a habit many fall into, can have a surprisingly profound negative impact on both personal and professional aspects of life. This chapter delves into the detrimental effects of perpetual negativity and how it can spiral into a self-fulfilling prophecy of dissatisfaction and missed opportunities. It's about recognizing the power of our words and thoughts and choosing a path that fosters positivity, growth, and empowerment.

The first and most visible impact of constant complaining is on our mental health. When we complain, we're essentially focusing on the negatives, often ignoring the positives that surround us. This negativity bias can lead to increased stress, anxiety, and even depression. It's a mental trap that paints our world in shades of gray, overshadowing the vibrant colors of joy and opportunity that exist in our lives.

Let's consider the story of Emily, a former colleague. Emily was known in the office for her constant complaints about work, from minor inconveniences to larger organizational issues. Over time, this habit began to shape her entire outlook. She became less engaged, her productivity dropped, and her ability to collaborate effectively with others diminished. Emily's case is a classic example of how constant complaining can create a toxic mindset, leading to a decrease in professional performance and job satisfaction.

The repercussions extend beyond our internal world. Constant complaining can strain relationships, both personal and professional. It can be exhausting for others to be around someone who frequently focuses on the negative. This can lead to social isolation, as people may start to distance themselves from the negative energy. In a professional setting, this can mean fewer collaborative opportunities, a decrease in trust from colleagues, and potentially stunted career growth.

Moreover, habitual complaining can blind us to opportunities for growth and problem-solving. Instead of seeking solutions or learning from challenges, a complainer often resigns themselves to a state of helplessness. This attitude not only hinders personal growth but also limits one's ability to contribute positively in a work environment.

The irony of constant complaining is that while it's often a plea for change or a better situation, it actively works against achieving those goals. The mindset that underpins complaining is one of powerlessness, which is in direct opposition to the mindset needed to effect change – that of empowerment and action.

Breaking free from the habit of constant complaining involves a conscious effort to shift one's focus and attitude. It's about practicing gratitude, engaging in positive self-talk, and adopting a problem-solving mindset. It's about recognizing that while we may not have control over every situation, we do have control over how we choose to respond.

The habit of constant complaining is a detrimental one, impacting our mental health, relationships, professional growth, and overall quality of life. By acknowledging the negative effects of this habit and actively working to shift our mindset, we can open ourselves up to a more positive, productive, and fulfilling life. Let's choose to focus on solutions, not problems, and embrace the power of a positive outlook to transform our personal and professional lives.

Turning Complaints into Solutions: A Shift in Mindset for Empowerment

Shifting from a complaint-based mindset to a solution-oriented approach is not just about changing how we think; it's about transforming how we live. This chapter explores practical strategies for making this pivotal shift, empowering us to tackle challenges with resilience and creativity, rather than falling into the trap of negativity and passivity.

The first step in this transformation is recognizing the nature of a complaint-based mindset. It often stems from a feeling of helplessness or frustration, focusing on problems rather than solutions. While it's natural to express dissatisfaction when things go awry, dwelling on these complaints without seeking solutions can lead to a negative spiral, impacting our mood, relationships, and even our health.

Let's consider the example of Sarah, a professional I once coached. Sarah often found herself complaining about her workload and the lack of support from her team. This constant negativity began to affect her performance and relationships at work. When Sarah learned to shift her focus from the problems to potential solutions, she not only improved her work environment but also gained recognition for her proactive approach.

Here are key strategies to facilitate this mindset shift:

1. Awareness and Pause: Recognize when you're about to complain. Pause and take a moment to reflect on what's driving this impulse. Is it a habitual response, or is there a valid concern that needs to be addressed?

2. Reframe the Narrative: Instead of saying, "This situation is terrible," try, "This situation is challenging, but I can handle it." This reframing shifts your perspective from victimhood to empowerment.

3. Focus on What You Can Control: Identify aspects of the situation that are within your control. Focusing on these elements can help you feel more empowered and less overwhelmed.

4. Seek Solutions: Once you've identified a problem, spend your energy brainstorming potential solutions. This proactive approach not only addresses the issue at hand but also fosters a sense of competence and effectiveness.

5. Practice Gratitude: Cultivating gratitude can help counterbalance the negativity of complaining. Regularly acknowledging what you're thankful for shifts your focus from what's going wrong to what's going right.

6. Solicit Feedback and Ideas: Sometimes, finding a solution requires outside perspectives. Don't hesitate to ask for feedback or ideas from others, as this can provide new insights and approaches.

7. Take Action: Once you've identified a possible solution, take action. Even small steps towards addressing the issue can make a significant difference in your mindset and situation.

Shifting from a complaint-based mindset to a solution-oriented approach is a powerful change that can profoundly impact your personal and professional life. This shift is not just about stopping complaints; it's about transforming them into opportunities for growth, learning, and empowerment. By adopting this approach, you become an active participant in shaping your life's narrative, steering it towards positivity, effectiveness, and fulfillment. Remember, every complaint holds the seed of a potential solution – it's up to you to nurture it into fruition.

Cultivating Gratitude and Positivity: Techniques for an Empowered Mindset

In the pursuit of a fulfilling life, the power of gratitude and positive thinking cannot be overstated. These are not just feel-good concepts but transformative tools that can reshape our perspective, improve our mental well-being, and open doors to new possibilities. This chapter is dedicated to practical techniques for cultivating gratitude and fostering a positive mindset, helping us to navigate life's ups and downs with resilience and optimism.

The first step in this transformative journey is understanding the profound impact gratitude and positivity can have on our lives. A grateful mindset shifts our focus from what we lack to what we possess, filling us with a sense of abundance and contentment. Positive thinking, on the other hand, doesn't mean ignoring life's challenges; rather, it's about approaching difficulties with a hopeful and constructive attitude.

Let's explore some practical techniques to cultivate these powerful states of mind:

1. Gratitude Journaling: Start or end your day by writing down three things you are grateful for. These can be as simple as a sunny day, a good conversation, or a productive work session. This practice trains your brain to recognize and appreciate the positive aspects of your life, even on tough days.

2. Positive Affirmations: Incorporate positive affirmations into your daily routine. Affirmations like "I am capable of overcoming challenges" or "I welcome positivity into my life" can boost self-esteem and foster a positive mindset. Say them out loud, write them down, or even place sticky notes around your home and workspace as reminders.

3. Mindfulness and Meditation: Engage in mindfulness or meditation practices. These can help you stay present and reduce negative or anxious thoughts. Even just a few minutes a day can make a significant difference in your mental state.

4. Acts of Kindness: Perform small acts of kindness. Helping others not only brings joy to those you assist but also boosts your own mood and fosters a sense of gratitude and connection.

5. Positive Environment: Surround yourself with positivity. This includes engaging with positive people, consuming uplifting content, and creating an environment that reflects a positive and grateful mindset.

6. Reframe Challenges: When faced with challenges, try to reframe them as opportunities for learning and growth. Ask yourself, "What can I learn from this situation?" instead of dwelling on the negative aspects.

7. Celebrate Small Wins: Acknowledge and celebrate your achievements, no matter how small. This practice reinforces a positive mindset and motivates you to keep moving forward.

8. Visualization: Spend time visualizing your goals and the positive outcomes you desire. This visualization can be a powerful motivator and helps in maintaining a positive outlook.

Cultivating gratitude and a positive mindset is a journey, not a destination. It requires consistent practice and a conscious choice to focus on the brighter side of life. By integrating these techniques into your daily life, you can transform your mindset, enhance your well-being, and open yourself up to a world of new possibilities. Remember, the power to shape your perspective and, in turn, your reality, lies within you. Embrace these practices, and watch as your life unfolds in more joyful and fulfilling ways.

From Complaining to Empowering: Real-Life Transformations

In our journey through life, the transformation from a mindset mired in complaints to one that is proactive and empowering is both challenging and incredibly rewarding. This chapter celebrates real-life stories of individuals who have made this profound shift, turning their habitual complaints into proactive steps towards a better life. These narratives not only inspire but also demonstrate the power of decision-making, the impact of small changes, and the resilience of the human spirit in overcoming habitual negativity.

One such story is of Clara, a client I once worked with. Clara was known in her office as the chronic complainer, always finding fault with her colleagues, the management, and the overall working conditions. This negative outlook started to affect her professional relationships and career growth. The turning point came when Clara attended a workshop that emphasized the power of positive thinking and proactive behavior. She began to implement small changes in her daily routine, such as starting her day with a list of things she was grateful for and replacing each complaint with a solution-oriented statement. Over time, these small steps led to a significant shift in her mindset. Clara transformed from a chronic complainer to a valued team member known for her constructive feedback and problem-solving skills. Her career trajectory took a positive turn, and she found greater satisfaction in her work.

Another inspiring example is that of Michael, a friend who once viewed life through a lens of negativity. His constant complaints about everything, from his health to his relationships, left him isolated and unhappy. The catalyst for change was a health scare that forced him to reevaluate his outlook on life. Michael realized that his complaining was not only unproductive but also harmful to his well-being. He decided to take charge of his life. He started exercising, eating healthier, and actively sought out positive experiences and people. He also began volunteering, which shifted his focus from his problems to helping others with theirs. This new proactive approach brought about a remarkable change in Michael's life, improving his health, relationships, and overall happiness.

These stories highlight a crucial lesson: the way we talk about our lives shapes our experiences. By shifting from a habit of complaining to one of proactive thinking, individuals like Clara and Michael have not only improved their own lives but also positively influenced those around them.

The transformation from chronic complaining to proactive living involves several key steps: recognizing the negative impact of constant complaining, consciously choosing to focus on solutions, practicing gratitude, seeking positive influences, and taking action to make positive changes.

The journey from a complaint-based mindset to a proactive approach is one of empowerment and growth. It's about taking control of our narrative and making conscious decisions that positively impact our life trajectory. The stories of Clara, Michael, and many others serve as powerful reminders that change is possible and that we all have the capacity to reshape our lives through our thoughts, words, and actions. Let these transformations inspire you to examine your own mindset and embrace the empowering path of positivity and proactive change.

Embracing Responsibility: Exercises for Positive Action and Growth

Embracing responsibility and taking positive action are pivotal steps towards self-empowerment and fulfillment. This chapter presents practical exercises designed to cultivate a sense of responsibility and foster a habit of positive action. These exercises are not just about making better decisions; they're about transforming your approach to life, enabling you to take control of your destiny and drive meaningful change.

1. The Decision Diary

Start by keeping a Decision Diary for one week. Each day, write down all the decisions you make, big or small. At the end of each day, reflect on these decisions. Ask yourself: Were these decisions in line with your values and goals? How did they impact you and those around you? This exercise heightens your awareness of your decision-making process, helping you understand the impact of your choices and encouraging more deliberate and responsible decision-making.

2. The Gratitude Practice

Every morning, list three things you're grateful for. These can be simple, everyday things. This practice shifts your focus from what you lack to what you have, fostering a mindset of abundance and positivity. It also encourages you to recognize the role you play in creating positive aspects of your life, reinforcing a sense of responsibility for your own happiness.

3. The 'Can-Do' Action Plan

Create a daily 'Can-Do' Action Plan. Write down three small, achievable actions that align with your goals. Focus on actions that you have direct control over. This plan helps translate responsibility into tangible actions, building confidence in your ability to effect change in your life.

4. The Reflection Exercise

At the end of each week, spend some time reflecting on your experiences. Consider moments when you felt empowered or disempowered. What role did your own actions or decisions play in these situations? This reflection encourages you to recognize your power in shaping your life's narrative.

5. The Compliment Swap

For one week, every time you find yourself about to complain, switch it to a compliment or a statement of gratitude. This exercise helps shift your mindset from focusing on problems to appreciating what's working well, a key aspect of taking positive action.

6. The Solution Challenge

Whenever you face a problem, challenge yourself to come up with at least three potential solutions. This approach shifts your mindset from a problem-oriented to a solution-oriented one, highlighting your role in navigating challenges.

7. The Positive Influence Audit

Take stock of the people you spend the most time with and the content you consume. Are these influences positive or negative? Make a conscious decision to seek out positive influences, which can inspire and motivate you to take responsible and positive actions.

These exercises are designed to foster a mindset of responsibility and positive action. By integrating these practices into your daily life, you empower yourself to make decisions that align with your goals, take actions that drive positive change, and embrace the power you have to shape your life. Remember, the path to empowerment is paved with the small, consistent steps you take each day towards living a life of responsibility and positive action.

Chapter 10

Inner Strength in Adversity: The Pillars of Resilience

Adversity is an inescapable part of the human experience, yet within it lies the potential for extraordinary growth and development. This chapter delves into the concept of inner strength and resilience, exploring how these qualities can be cultivated and harnessed to not only navigate life's challenges but to emerge stronger and more empowered. It's about understanding that resilience isn't inherent; it's built through our responses to the difficulties we face.

Inner strength is the fortitude that allows us to face adversity without losing ourselves. It's a combination of mental, emotional, and spiritual toughness that provides the backbone for resilience. Resilience, on the other hand, is the ability to bounce back from setbacks, adapt to change, and keep going in the face of adversity. Together, these qualities create a formidable force, enabling us to handle life's ups and downs with grace and determination.

Let's explore the key components of building inner strength and resilience:

1. Self-Awareness: Recognizing your emotions and understanding your thoughts is the first step in building resilience. Self-awareness allows you to navigate your feelings and choose your responses more wisely.

2. Positive Mindset: Maintaining a positive outlook is crucial. This doesn't mean ignoring the negatives, but rather choosing to focus on the positives. It's about viewing challenges as opportunities for growth and learning.

3. Embracing Change: Change is inevitable. Embracing it as a part of life rather than resisting it is a key aspect of resilience. Flexibility and

adaptability are essential skills in managing change effectively.

4. Support Networks: Building strong relationships and having a support network can significantly boost your resilience. Knowing you have people to rely on can provide comfort and strength in tough times.

5. Problem-Solving Skills: Developing effective problem-solving skills helps you to deal with challenges more efficiently. It's about approaching problems with a calm, clear head and a can-do attitude.

6. Self-Care: Taking care of your physical, emotional, and mental well-being is crucial. Regular exercise, a healthy diet, adequate sleep, and stress-reduction activities like meditation can strengthen your resilience.

7. Goal-Setting: Having clear goals gives you direction and purpose, even in tough times. Setting and working towards goals can provide a sense of

achievement and help maintain focus when faced with adversity.

To illustrate these principles, consider the story of Maya, a young woman who faced significant personal and professional challenges. Through her journey, Maya learned the importance of self-awareness in recognizing her limits and the value of a support network. She embraced a positive mindset, viewing each setback as a learning opportunity. By focusing on self-care, setting realistic goals, and developing her problem-solving skills, Maya built her resilience, emerging stronger and more confident in her ability to handle future challenges.

Inner strength and resilience are not about never falling; they're about the courage to get back up every time we do. It's about using adversity as a catalyst for growth and transformation. By cultivating these qualities, we not only survive life's challenges but thrive in spite of them. Remember, resilience is a journey, not a destination, and every step you take towards building it is a step towards a more empowered and fulfilling life.

Fortifying the Mind and Heart: Techniques for Building Emotional and Mental Fortitude

Emotional and mental fortitude are like the compass and anchor that help us navigate turbulent seas with confidence and resilience. Building this inner strength is not just about enduring hard times; it's about thriving in the face of adversity. This chapter focuses on practical techniques for developing emotional and mental fortitude, emphasizing the power of small, consistent efforts in shaping a resilient mindset. It's about empowering you to take control of your emotional and mental well-being, transforming challenges into opportunities for growth.

1. Mindful Awareness:

Begin by cultivating mindfulness. This practice involves being fully present and aware of your thoughts and feelings without judgment. It allows you to observe your emotional responses and understand their triggers. You can start with just a few minutes a day, gradually increasing the time. Mindfulness helps in developing emotional regulation, a key component of mental fortitude.

2. Positive Self-Talk:

The language we use with ourselves significantly influences our mental and emotional state. Practice positive self-talk. Replace self-criticism with compassionate, encouraging words. Instead of saying, "I can't handle this," try, "I'm doing my best to cope with this situation." This shift in language reinforces a belief in your capabilities and resilience.

3. Emotional Expression and Processing:

Allow yourself to express and process your emotions. Bottling up feelings can lead to increased stress and anxiety. Find healthy outlets for emotional expression, such as journaling, talking with a trusted friend, or engaging in creative activities. This helps in acknowledging and understanding your emotions, building emotional resilience.

4. Stress Management Techniques:

Incorporate stress management techniques into your daily routine. This can include deep breathing exercises, meditation, yoga, or any physical activity that you enjoy.

Regular exercise not only helps in reducing stress but also boosts your mood and overall mental health.

5. Cultivate Gratitude:

Practice gratitude. Focus on the things you are thankful for, no matter how small. Gratitude shifts your focus from what you lack to what you have, fostering positivity and resilience.

6. Building a Support System:

Surround yourself with a strong support system. Having a network of friends, family, or mentors provides emotional support and perspective during tough times. It also reminds you that you are not alone in your struggles.

7. Continuous Learning and Growth Mindset:

Adopt a growth mindset. View challenges as opportunities for learning and personal development. Continuous learning and personal development are essential for building mental fortitude. Whether it's reading, taking courses, or engaging in new experiences, continuous learning broadens your perspective and strengthens your mental resilience.

8. Practice Resilience:

Finally, practice resilience actively. Setbacks and challenges are inevitable. Each time you face adversity, consciously apply these techniques. Reflect on your response, learn from the experience, and use this knowledge to handle future challenges more effectively.

Building emotional and mental fortitude is a dynamic and ongoing process. It requires patience, practice, and persistence. By integrating these techniques into your life, you empower yourself to face life's challenges with a stronger, more resilient mindset. Remember, the strength you need resides within you; it's just a matter of nurturing it through consistent practice and self-care.

Harnessing Mindset to Triumph Over Adversity

Where adversity often seems like an unyielding wave, there exists a singular, powerful tool within each of us – our mindset. The way we perceive and react to life's challenges is more than just a psychological state; it is the bedrock upon which we can build our triumphs. This concept, though seemingly simple, holds profound implications for how we navigate the turbulent waters of life.

Consider the story of Sarah, a young entrepreneur. When her first business venture failed, she was faced with two choices: to view this failure as a definitive end or as a vital lesson. By choosing the latter, Sarah transformed her setback into a stepping stone. This shift in perspective is the crux of overcoming adversity. It's not just about positive thinking; it's about harnessing the power of a resilient and adaptive mindset.

The role of mindset in overcoming adversity is not just about enduring hardships but about reshaping them into opportunities for growth. Life, much like a rigorous trainer, presents us with various obstacles, not to defeat us, but to strengthen us. Each challenge is an opportunity to test our resolve and adaptability. When we change our mindset, we change the game.

Let's talk about the power of decision-making. Every day, we are faced with countless decisions – some trivial, some life-altering. In these moments, our mindset can be our greatest ally or our most formidable foe. By approaching decisions with a mindset geared towards growth and learning, even the wrong choices become valuable lessons, not regrets.

Small changes in our daily approach can have a monumental impact on our overall life trajectory. Consider the habit of journaling. By simply taking a few minutes each day to reflect and write down our thoughts and experiences, we cultivate a practice of mindfulness and self-awareness. This seemingly small act can profoundly influence how we perceive and react to life's challenges.

Now, think about resilience. It's not an inherent trait but a skill that can be developed and strengthened over time, much like a muscle. Every time we choose to face our fears, to stand back up after a fall, we are exercising and fortifying our resilience. It's about embracing the discomfort of growth and recognizing that every challenge is a catalyst for personal development.

In essence, our mindset is the architect of our destiny. It shapes how we interpret our experiences, how we react to life's ups and downs, and ultimately, how we carve our path forward. By cultivating a mindset that views adversity not as a barrier but as a bridge to greater understanding and strength, we unlock our inherent power to overcome and thrive.

Remember that the journey of overcoming adversity is deeply personal and uniquely yours. Each challenge you face is a chapter in your story, a testament to your resilience and growth. Embrace your journey with a mindset focused on learning and growth, and watch as you transform obstacles into opportunities, and adversity into triumph.

Unyielding Spirit: Stories of Resilience from France

There lies a remarkable strength waiting to be uncovered. This truth is beautifully illustrated in the stories of individuals from France who found extraordinary strength during challenging times. Their journeys are not just tales of survival, but beacons of resilience, demonstrating the incredible power of the human spirit.

Take the story of Élise, a baker from a small town in Provence. When a sudden economic downturn threatened her family-owned bakery, Élise faced an uphill battle. Instead of succumbing to despair, she made a decision that altered her life's trajectory. She innovated, introducing a line of artisanal, locally-sourced pastries that revitalized her business. Élise's story isn't just about business acumen; it's a testament to the power of embracing change and making proactive decisions, even in the face of uncertainty.

Then, there's the narrative of Jacques, a teacher in Paris. When he was diagnosed with a chronic illness, his world turned upside down. But Jacques chose not to let his condition define him. He adopted small, daily habits that improved his well-being and continued to inspire his students with his unwavering dedication. His journey illustrates the impact of maintaining a positive mindset and making incremental changes that collectively forge a path to overcoming personal adversity.

Another inspiring tale comes from Amélie, a young athlete from Lyon. After a severe injury jeopardized her career, she faced what seemed like an insurmountable challenge. However, Amélie's story didn't end there. Through relentless determination and adapting her training regime, she not only recovered but returned to her sport stronger than ever. Her experience highlights the importance of resilience and the power of adapting to new circumstances.

These stories share a common thread – the incredible impact of decision-making in times of adversity. Each individual faced their challenges head-on, making choices that steered their lives in a new, positive direction. Their decisions, no matter how small they seemed at the time, accumulated into significant changes in their life trajectories.

It's crucial to recognize that resilience is not an innate trait but a skill that can be cultivated. Just like Élise, Jacques, and Amélie, each of us can develop this skill by embracing challenges as opportunities for growth. This mindset shift is essential for personal empowerment and overcoming adversity.

Remember, every challenge presents a chance to make a decision. Will you choose to see a setback as a dead end, or as an opportunity to learn and grow? The stories of these remarkable individuals from France serve as powerful reminders of what we can achieve when we approach life with courage, determination, and a positive mindset.

Let these stories inspire you. You have the same innate strength and resilience within you. With each decision you make, you have the power to shape your destiny. Embrace your journey with courage and optimism, and you too can turn adversity into an opportunity for personal growth and triumph.

Navigating Storms: Strategies for Composure and Clarity in Crises

In life, we are often thrown into the tumultuous seas of crises, where maintaining composure and clarity can feel like an insurmountable task. Yet, it's in these turbulent times that the strength of our resolve is truly tested, and our ability to navigate through them defines our journey. This piece is not just about surviving crises but thriving through them by harnessing practical, actionable strategies.

One of the first and most critical steps in a crisis is to ground yourself in the present moment. It's easy to get caught up in the 'what-ifs' and the chaos of an unraveling situation. Instead, take a deep breath, focus on your surroundings, and anchor yourself in the now. This simple act of mindfulness creates a mental space of clarity, allowing you to assess the situation more objectively.

Remember the story of Laura, a nurse who worked during a major health crisis. Amidst the chaos, she found her grounding by focusing on one task at a time. This approach didn't just help her navigate the crisis effectively but also made her a pillar of strength for her colleagues. Laura's story underscores the importance of tackling challenges in bite-sized pieces, preventing the overwhelming feeling that often accompanies crises.

Another crucial strategy is to maintain a problem-solving mindset. Crises are inherently filled with problems that need solving. By adopting a mindset that views challenges as solvable puzzles, you shift from a state of panic to one of empowerment. Think about how Max, a small business owner, faced the brink of bankruptcy. Instead of succumbing to defeat, he viewed each obstacle as a problem to be solved, ultimately steering his business through rough waters to safe harbor.

Emotional regulation is also key in times of crisis. It's natural to experience a rollercoaster of emotions, but it's essential to manage these emotions effectively. Practice self-compassion and allow yourself to feel these emotions, but also strive to keep them from clouding your judgment. Techniques such as deep breathing, meditation, or even a simple walk can help in regaining emotional equilibrium.

Moreover, don't underestimate the power of seeking support. Crises can make us feel isolated, but remember, you're not alone. Reach out to friends, family, or professional counselors. Sharing your burdens not only lightens your load but also opens up new perspectives that you might have missed.

Finally, learn from the crisis. Every crisis, no matter how daunting, is a learning opportunity. Reflect on what worked, what didn't, and how you can be better prepared for future challenges. This reflective practice not only builds resilience but also turns crises into valuable lessons.

Remember that crises, while challenging, are not the end. They are turning points, opportunities to grow, learn, and emerge stronger. By staying present, tackling problems one at a time, regulating emotions, seeking support, and learning from the experience, you can navigate any storm with composure and clarity. So, embrace these strategies, empower yourself, and turn your crises into stepping stones for personal growth and resilience.

Building Inner Strength: Exercises for Resilience

The development of a resilient and strong inner self is akin to building a fortress within, one that stands steadfast against the storms of adversity and change. This process, while challenging, is deeply rewarding and transformative.

By integrating practical exercises into our daily routines, we can fortify our inner strength and cultivate resilience that endures.

Firstly, let's talk about the power of positive self-talk. The language we use with ourselves shapes our mindset and beliefs. Start by becoming aware of your inner dialogue. Is it encouraging or critical? Transform negative self-talk into positive affirmations. For example, replace thoughts like "I can't handle this" with "I am capable and strong." This simple shift can have a profound impact on your confidence and resilience.

A real-life example of this is Anna, a teacher who struggled with self-doubt. By consciously changing her inner dialogue, she not only improved her self-esteem but also became a more effective and inspiring teacher. Her story illustrates how small changes in our self-talk can lead to significant transformations in our personal and professional lives.

Another vital exercise is practicing gratitude. In the hustle of everyday life, it's easy to overlook the good around us. Take a few minutes each day to reflect on what you're grateful for. This practice fosters positivity and helps in building a resilient mindset. Gratitude shifts our focus from what's lacking to what's abundant, reinforcing a sense of contentment and strength.

Mindfulness and meditation are also key exercises in developing inner strength. These practices help in cultivating a sense of calm and centeredness, especially important during times of stress or crisis. Start with just a few minutes a day, focusing on your breath or engaging in guided meditation. The goal is to create a space of inner peace that you can return to, regardless of external circumstances.

Journaling is another powerful tool. It's a way to process emotions, reflect on experiences, and gain clarity. Set aside time each day to write down your thoughts, feelings, and reflections. This practice not only provides emotional release but also helps in tracking your personal growth and understanding your resilience journey.

Additionally, setting and achieving small goals is an excellent way to build inner strength. Goals give us direction and a sense of purpose. Start with small, achievable targets and gradually increase the challenge. Celebrate your successes along the way, no matter how small. This process builds confidence and reinforces the belief in your abilities.

Finally, fostering connections with others is crucial. Building supportive relationships provides a safety net for when times get tough. Sharing your journey, learning from others, and offering support not only strengthens your resilience but also enriches your life with meaningful connections.

Developing a resilient and strong inner self is a journey that requires patience, persistence, and practice. Through positive self-talk, gratitude, mindfulness, journaling, goal setting, and fostering connections, you can build an inner fortress of strength and resilience. Remember, the power to grow and thrive lies within you. Embrace these exercises, empower yourself, and watch as you transform challenges into opportunities for growth and strength.

Chapter 11

The Conscious Choice – Shaping Your Life with Intention

At the heart of a fulfilling life lies the power of conscious decision-making. It's about understanding that each choice we make, big or small, shapes our life experiences. This chapter isn't just about choices; it's about empowering yourself to be the architect of your own destiny.

Let's start with a fundamental truth: every day, we're inundated with decisions. From the moment we wake up to when we close our eyes at night, our lives are a series of choices. Some seem insignificant, like choosing what to wear or what to cat for breakfast. Others feel monumental, determining the course of our careers, relationships, and personal well-being. But here's the catch – even the smallest decisions can have a profound impact on our life trajectory.

Take the story of Emma, for example. She was stuck in a job that drained her, both emotionally and creatively. Every day, she faced a choice: stay in the comfort of the known or take a leap into the unknown. It was a small, conscious decision to update her resume and apply for a new job that set her on a path to a fulfilling career. Emma's story illustrates that sometimes, the smallest step can lead to the biggest change.

Now, consider the impact of habitual decisions – the ones we make daily without much thought. These choices accumulate, forming the foundation of our routines, habits, and ultimately, our lives. Imagine if you choose to spend just ten minutes a day learning a new skill or exercising. Over a year, that's over sixty hours dedicated to self-improvement. This example underscores the cumulative power of small, consistent choices.

Making conscious choices also means being mindful of the present moment. It's easy to get caught up in past regrets or future anxieties, but real power lies in the now. When you're fully present, your decisions are more deliberate and informed. This mindfulness creates a space where you can weigh your options, consider potential outcomes, and choose a path that aligns with your values and goals.

But what about the tough choices, the ones that challenge us to our core? Here's where the true strength of conscious decision-making comes into play. It's in these moments that you have to tap into your inner resilience and wisdom. Remember, challenging decisions often lead to the most significant growth. They push us out of our comfort zones and force us to confront our fears and uncertainties.

In embracing conscious decision-making, it's crucial to accept that not all choices will lead to the desired outcome. This is where resilience comes in. It's not about making the perfect choice every time; it's about learning from each decision and moving forward with newfound knowledge and insight.

The power of conscious decision-making cannot be overstated. Every choice you make is a building block in the construction of your life. By making decisions mindfully and intentionally, you take control of your destiny. So, embrace the power of The Conscious Choice. Recognize that in every decision lies an opportunity to shape your life in the direction of your dreams. Remember, your life is a masterpiece, and you hold the brush.

Proactive vs. Reactive: Mastering Your Responses

Our responses to situations paint the colors of our experiences. Understanding and differentiating between reactive and proactive responses can be a game-changer in how we navigate life's challenges and opportunities. This chapter isn't just about responses; it's about empowering you to respond in ways that enrich your life.

Let's start with reactive responses. Imagine you're driving, and suddenly someone cuts you off. Your immediate reaction is anger, perhaps honking the horn or yelling. This is a reactive response, driven by emotion, often without considering the long-term effects. It's an instinctual, sometimes impulsive reaction to external stimuli. While it's natural to react this way, it's not always beneficial. Reactive responses can lead to stress, conflict, and missed opportunities for more thoughtful engagement.

Now, let's explore proactive responses. Picture the same scenario, but this time, when someone cuts you off, you take a deep breath and choose not to react in anger. Instead, you focus on driving safely and let the moment pass. This is a proactive response. It's a conscious, deliberate choice, made by assessing the situation and considering the best course of action. Proactive responses are grounded in thoughtfulness and often aligned with long-term goals and values.

Think about Sarah, a manager in a fast-paced office. When faced with unexpected challenges, she used to react immediately, often leading to increased stress for her and her team. However, by shifting to a proactive approach, Sarah started to assess situations before responding. This shift not only improved her decision-making but also created a more positive, productive work environment.

The difference between reactive and proactive responses lies in control. In reactive mode, our environment controls us. We're at the mercy of external events. In contrast, proactive responses put us in the driver's seat. We control our responses, not the other way around.

So, how do you cultivate a proactive mindset? It starts with awareness. Recognize your typical reactions in various situations. Do you respond with immediacy and emotion, or do you take a moment to process and decide the best course of action?

Practicing mindfulness can be incredibly effective. It helps you stay grounded in the present moment, making you more aware of your reactions. When you're mindful, you create a space between stimulus and response. In this space lies your power to choose a proactive response.

Setting clear goals and values also guides proactive responses. When you know what you stand for and where you want to go, your decisions and responses will naturally align with your goals.

The shift from reactive to proactive responses is not just about changing how you react; it's about changing how you live. By choosing proactive responses, you take control of your life's narrative. You move from being a passive reactor to an active creator of your life story. Embrace this shift, and watch as you transform challenges into opportunities, stress into peace, and impulsivity into thoughtful action. Remember, in every moment, you have the power to choose, and in that choice lies your freedom and growth.

Everyday Mindfulness: Cultivating Awareness in Daily Life

Integrating mindfulness into our daily routines is not just attainable; it's transformative. This chapter isn't about grand gestures or complete lifestyle overhauls. It's about simple, practical strategies to bring mindfulness into your everyday life, empowering you to live more fully, consciously, and joyfully.

First and foremost, understand that mindfulness is the art of being fully present and engaged in the moment, without judgment. It's about experiencing life as it unfolds, with an open and accepting attitude. The beauty of mindfulness is that it can be practiced anywhere, anytime. It's not confined to meditation cushions or yoga mats; it's accessible in every breath, step, and moment.

One of the most straightforward ways to cultivate mindfulness is through focused breathing. It sounds simple, yet its impact is profound. Try this: several times a day, pause for a minute or two and concentrate solely on your breathing. Notice the sensation of air entering and leaving your body, the rise and fall of your chest or abdomen. This practice can anchor you in the present moment, calm your mind, and refocus your attention.

Let's take the example of John, a busy professional. Amidst his hectic schedule, he found himself constantly stressed and distracted. By incorporating short breathing exercises into his daily routine – during his morning commute, before meetings, and after work – John began to experience a greater sense of calm and focus. This small change had a ripple effect, enhancing his productivity and overall well-being.

Another effective strategy is the practice of mindful eating. Often, we eat on autopilot, not really tasting or enjoying our food. Try eating one meal a day mindfully. Turn off the TV, put away your phone, and really focus on your meal. Savor each bite, notice the textures, the flavors, the aromas. Mindful eating not only enhances the enjoyment of your meal but also improves digestion and fosters a healthier relationship with food.

Incorporating mindfulness into your daily routines can also be transformative. Take regular activities like showering, walking, or doing dishes. Instead of rushing through these tasks, use them as opportunities to practice mindfulness. Pay attention to the sensations, the sounds, the movements. This approach can turn mundane activities into moments of peace and awareness.

Mindfulness can also be cultivated through reflection and gratitude. Spend a few minutes at the end of each day reflecting on what you are thankful for. Acknowledge the good in your life, the successes of the day, no matter how small. This practice not only fosters a positive mindset but also grounds you in the present, helping you appreciate the richness of your life.

Mindfulness is not a destination; it's a journey. It's about finding moments of awareness in the chaos of everyday life. By practicing focused breathing, mindful eating, integrating mindfulness into daily routines, and reflecting on gratitude, you can cultivate a more mindful, present, and fulfilling life. Remember, the journey to mindfulness begins with a single, conscious breath. Start there, and watch as the magic unfolds.

Transformative Choices: French Tales of Triumph

In the heart of France, a country known for its rich history and vibrant culture, there are individuals whose life stories stand as powerful testaments to the impact of conscious choices. These narratives aren't just about success; they are about transformation, resilience, and the profound influence of deliberate decision-making on the trajectory of one's life. Each story is a mosaic of choices, small and large, that collectively sculpt a journey of empowerment and achievement.

Take the story of Claire, a Parisian artist. For years, she worked in a conventional office job, feeling unfulfilled and disconnected from her passion for painting. The turning point came when she made the conscious choice to follow her heart. Despite the risks, Claire transitioned to a full-time artist. This decision wasn't made in a day; it involved small, incremental steps – attending evening art classes, building a portfolio, and gradually shifting her career path. Today, Claire's artwork is showcased in galleries across France, a living testament to the power of aligning choices with one's passions.

Then there's Marc, a chef from Lyon, who transformed his health through conscious lifestyle choices. Struggling with weight and health issues, Marc decided to overhaul his diet and exercise regimen. This choice went beyond mere dieting; it was about a lifestyle change. Marc started sourcing local, healthy ingredients and incorporating them into his recipes. This journey wasn't easy, especially in the culinary world known for rich foods, but Marc's dedication led to not only a personal transformation but also influenced his professional style, leading to a successful health-focused restaurant.

Another inspiring story comes from Sophie, a teacher in Marseille. Sophie faced educational challenges in her community and saw that traditional teaching methods weren't addressing students' needs. She made a series of choices to integrate innovative teaching techniques, despite skepticism from peers. Her decisions were rooted in a deep belief in every child's potential. Sophie's proactive approach resulted in significantly improved student engagement and performance, changing many young lives.

These stories from France share a common theme: the remarkable impact of conscious decision-making. Each individual faced a point where they had to choose between the familiarity of the status quo and the uncertainty of change. In making intentional choices, aligned with their values and aspirations, they transformed their lives.

What these stories teach us is the power of decision-making in shaping our lives. Whether it's a career change, a health transformation, or an educational revolution, the decisions we make can lead to profound personal and professional transformations. The journey of change begins with a single choice, a conscious step towards the life you desire.

The tales of Claire, Marc, and Sophie are not just success stories; they are a call to action. They remind us that we hold the power to change our lives through our choices. So, embrace the power of conscious decision-making. Remember, each choice you make is a brushstroke in the masterpiece of your life. Make those choices count.

Decision Dynamics: Enhancing Your Choice-Making Skills

The skill of making sound, effective decisions is more vital than ever. This chapter delves into practical techniques for enhancing decision-making skills, empowering you to navigate life's crossroads with confidence and clarity. It's about transforming the daunting task of decision-making into an empowering process that propels you towards your goals.

Firstly, let's acknowledge a fundamental truth: decision-making is not just about choosing between right and wrong. It's about evaluating options, considering potential outcomes, and aligning choices with your goals and values. The key to enhanced decision-making lies in understanding that it's a skill you can develop and refine.

One effective technique is the practice of informed reflection. Before making a decision, gather as much information as possible. Educate yourself about the options and understand their potential consequences. Think about Julia, a graphic designer who wanted to start her own business. Before taking the leap, she spent months researching the market, understanding her competition, and evaluating her financial readiness. This informed approach gave her the clarity and confidence to make the right decision.

Another crucial aspect is learning to trust your intuition. Sometimes, amidst all the logical analysis, what you need is to listen to your inner voice. Your intuition is shaped by your experiences and values, and often, it guides you towards choices that are true to yourself. Remember, intuition and logic are not mutually exclusive; they can and should work together in the decision-making process.

Embracing the power of pros and cons lists is another practical approach. This time-tested method involves writing down the advantages and disadvantages of each option. This simple act of listing can provide a clear visual representation of your choices, making it easier to weigh them against each other. It's a method that brings clarity to complex situations.

One often overlooked technique is setting a deadline for your decision. Indecision can be a decision in itself, and usually not a productive one. Setting a deadline forces you to actively engage with the decision-making process and prevents procrastination. It creates a sense of urgency that can help clarify your thoughts.

Additionally, don't underestimate the value of seeking diverse perspectives. Consult with people whose opinions you respect – friends, family, mentors. They can provide insights that you might have overlooked. However, remember that the final decision rests with you. Use these insights as guidance, not gospel.

Lastly, embrace the learning process. Not every decision will lead to the desired outcome, and that's okay. Each choice is an opportunity to learn and grow. Reflect on your decisions, understand what worked and what didn't, and use these insights to refine your decision-making skills.

Enhancing your decision-making skills is about adopting a holistic approach. It involves informed reflection, trusting your intuition, making pros and cons lists, setting deadlines, seeking diverse perspectives, and learning from each decision. Remember, at the heart of powerful decision-making lies a balance between logic and intuition, analysis and action. Embrace these techniques, and watch as you navigate the path of life with greater confidence and clarity.

The Art of Conscious Choice: A Guide to Empowered Decision-Making

The steps we take are often dictated by the choices we make. Developing conscious choice-making isn't just about selecting between options; it's about embracing a practice that aligns your decisions with your true self and life goals. This chapter is a guided journey into the art of conscious choice-making, a path that leads to empowered and fulfilling decision-making.

The first step in this journey is cultivating self-awareness. Self-awareness is the cornerstone of conscious decision-making. It involves understanding your values, goals, and the factors that influence your choices. Start with a simple exercise: spend a few minutes each day reflecting on your decisions. Ask yourself, "Why did I make this choice? Does it align with my values and goals?" Over time, this practice will sharpen your awareness of your decision-making patterns and motivations.

Next, let's delve into the power of visualization. Visualization is a potent tool for conscious decision-making. Before making a choice, take a moment to visualize the outcomes of each option. Picture not just the immediate effects, but also the long-term impact on your life. Visualization helps in creating a mental roadmap of where each choice could lead. It's a technique that brings clarity and foresight into the decision-making process.

Another key practice is learning to listen to your intuition. Often, our gut feelings give us a clear sense of what is right for us. However, in the noise of external opinions and internal conflicts, this intuitive voice can get lost. Dedicate time to quieten your mind, perhaps through meditation or a walk in nature, and tune into your inner voice. Remember, intuition is not about impulsive reactions;

it's a deeper sense of knowing that comes from aligning with your core self.

Incorporating mindfulness into your decision-making process is also essential. Mindfulness means being fully present in the moment, aware of yourself and your surroundings. When faced with a decision, practice mindfulness to bring your full attention to the choices at hand. This can be as simple as taking a few deep breaths before deciding, ensuring that you are grounded and centered.

It's also crucial to adopt a growth mindset. Understand that every choice, whether successful or not, is an opportunity to learn and grow. Approach decision-making with curiosity and openness to new experiences. Embrace the possibility that even less favorable outcomes have valuable lessons.

Finally, develop a habit of reflecting on your decisions. After making a choice, take time to reflect on its outcomes. Did it bring you closer to your goals? Did it align with your values? Reflection is a powerful tool for learning and growth in the art of decision-making.

Conscious choice-making is a practice that can be developed through self-awareness, visualization, intuition, mindfulness, a growth mindset, and reflective practices. It's about making decisions that are not just reactive responses to external circumstances but deliberate choices that reflect your true self and aspirations. Embrace these practices, and step into a life where each choice you make is a conscious step towards the life you envision.

Chapter 12

Beyond Beginnings – Understanding Upbringing and Moving Forward

Our upbringing is the first chapter in our life story, laying the foundation upon which we build our adult lives. This chapter delves into the complex tapestry of how our early experiences shape our behaviors and choices as adults, and more importantly, how we can move beyond our beginnings to craft our own narratives.

The environment we grow up in, the values instilled in us, the relationships we observe and engage in – all these aspects of our upbringing play a pivotal role in molding our adult personas. They influence our belief systems, our reactions to stress, our coping mechanisms, and our decision-making patterns. Recognizing this influence is the first step in understanding ourselves and steering our life's course more consciously.

Consider the story of Alex, who grew up in a family where financial instability was a constant. This upbringing ingrained in him a deep-seated fear of financial insecurity. As an adult, this fear manifested in Alex being overly cautious and sometimes missing out on potentially rewarding opportunities. It wasn't until Alex acknowledged this pattern and understood its roots in his upbringing that he could begin to address it, learning to balance caution with calculated risks.

However, while our upbringing significantly influences us, it does not determine our destiny. We are not bound by our past. The beauty of adulthood lies in the ability to make choices, to change patterns, and to grow beyond the limits of our early environments. This is where the power of conscious decision-making comes into play, allowing us to reshape our lives regardless of our beginnings.

It's crucial to recognize the small, everyday choices that lead to significant changes over time. Small steps, like seeking new experiences, challenging long-held beliefs, or even changing our response to familiar situations, can have a profound impact on our life trajectory.

Mindfulness and self-reflection are key tools in this process. By being mindful, we become aware of our automatic responses and behaviors that stem from our upbringing. This awareness is the first step in changing those patterns. Reflecting on why we react a certain way or make certain choices can open doors to new ways of thinking and being.

Another essential aspect is seeking external perspectives and support when needed. Sometimes, talking to a friend, a mentor, or a professional can provide insights that we might be too close to see. These perspectives can help us understand the impact of our upbringing and guide us in moving forward.

Our upbringing plays a significant role in shaping who we are, but it doesn't have to define who we become. By acknowledging and understanding the influence of our early years, making conscious choices, practicing mindfulness, and seeking growth and support, we can move beyond our beginnings. Remember, you are the author of your life story. Use the pen of conscious choice-making to write a narrative of growth, resilience, and empowerment, no matter what your first chapters looked like.

Bridging Past and Future: The Art of Balanced Acknowledgment

Life is a delicate dance between reflecting on what has been and focusing on what can be. This chapter delves into the art of balancing acknowledgment of the past with a focus on the future. It's about harnessing the lessons of yesterday to fuel the dreams of tomorrow, without getting lost in the echoes of what once was.

Acknowledging the past is crucial. Our histories are rich tapestries of experiences that shape our identities and perspectives. However, dwelling excessively on past events, especially those that are painful or regretful, can tether us to a static identity, hindering growth and progress. The key lies in embracing the past without letting it dominate our present or dictate our future.

Consider the story of Elena, a talented musician. For years, she was held back by a past failure at a major performance. This single event overshadowed her perception of her abilities. It was only when Elena began to view her past experience as a learning opportunity that she could move forward. She took lessons from that failure – what went wrong, what she could have done differently – and used them to improve her craft. Elena's story illustrates that the past need not be a shadow but can be a guiding light.

Balancing this acknowledgment with a focus on the future involves intentional decision-making. Each day presents opportunities to make choices that align with our future goals. It's about being proactive, setting goals, and taking steps, however small, towards achieving them. This future-focused approach doesn't ignore the past; rather, it builds upon it.

Practicing mindfulness is a powerful tool in this balancing act. Mindfulness keeps us anchored in the present, the bridge between our past and future. It enables us to appreciate our past experiences for their lessons and use the present moment as a launching pad for future aspirations. Through mindfulness, we can acknowledge where we have been while staying focused on where we are going.

Additionally, visualization can be a transformative practice. Visualize where you want to be – what does your future look like? How does it differ from your past? Visualization not only creates a clear picture of your goals but also motivates and directs your daily choices towards achieving them.

Let's not forget the role of resilience. The journey from past to future is rarely linear or smooth. It requires resilience – the ability to bounce back from setbacks and keep moving forward. Resilience is fueled by both the strength drawn from past experiences and the optimism for the future.

Balancing acknowledgment of the past with a focus on the future is a dynamic and ongoing process. It requires mindfulness, proactive decision-making, visualization, and resilience. Remember, your past is a rich repository of lessons, not a blueprint for your future. Use these lessons as a foundation to build a future that resonates with your aspirations and dreams. The past is your teacher, the future your canvas – paint it with the colors of growth, purpose, and hope.

Breaking Free: Overcoming Negative Family Patterns

This section is about breaking free from these cycles, not with resentment or blame, but with understanding, resilience, and empowerment. It's about creating a new legacy for yourself, one that aligns with who you are and who you aspire to be.

The first step in breaking free from negative family patterns is recognizing and acknowledging them. This requires introspection and honesty. It's about identifying the behaviors, attitudes, or beliefs within your family that are detrimental to your well-being and growth. Consider the story of Mia, who grew up in a family where expressing emotions was discouraged. As an adult, she found it challenging to form deep, emotional connections. It was only when Mia acknowledged this pattern that she could begin to work on expressing her emotions more openly.

Once you've recognized these patterns, the next step is understanding their origins. This isn't about placing blame but about comprehending the context in which these behaviors were learned. Understanding provides a compassionate lens through which to view these patterns. It's similar to putting together a puzzle – understanding each piece's place helps make sense of the whole picture.

The power of decision-making then comes into play. Each day we make choices that either perpetuate these negative patterns or break free from them. It's about making conscious decisions that align with your values and the life you want to lead. This could involve setting boundaries, seeking professional help, or consciously adopting healthier behaviors. Remember, change starts with a decision – your decision.

Creating a support system is crucial. Surround yourself with people who support and encourage your journey. These could be friends, mentors, or support groups. They provide an external perspective and can offer encouragement and advice when you're struggling to break free from negative patterns.

Another strategy is to practice new behaviors. This is where the impact of small changes becomes evident. Adopting new behaviors, even in small ways, can start to shift these patterns. If communication was a challenge in your family, start by expressing your thoughts and feelings in safe, supportive environments. Over time, these small changes accumulate, creating a new pattern of behavior.

Mindfulness and self-compassion are also key in this process. Be mindful of when you fall into old patterns and approach these moments with self-compassion. Change isn't easy, and it doesn't happen overnight. Treat yourself with kindness and understanding as you navigate this journey.

Breaking free from negative family patterns is a journey of self-discovery, resilience, and empowerment. It involves recognizing and understanding these patterns, making conscious choices, building a supportive network, practicing new behaviors, and approaching the journey with mindfulness and self-compassion. Remember, you have the power to rewrite your story. Each choice you make is a step towards breaking free and creating a legacy that reflects your true self.

Rising Above: Inspirational Journeys Beyond Upbringing

Each individual's journey through life is uniquely their own, yet some stories stand out as beacons of inspiration, demonstrating the incredible power of transcending one's upbringing. These narratives are not just about overcoming adversity; they are profound examples of resilience, determination, and the transformative power of choice. This chapter celebrates the stories of individuals who, despite their challenging upbringings, chose to forge their own paths and redefine their destinies.

Let's start with the story of Leo, who grew up in a small, economically challenged town. His early life was marked by hardship and limited opportunities. However, Leo refused to let his circumstances define his future. He pursued education with fervor, using every resource available, from public libraries to online courses. His journey wasn't easy, filled with long nights and sacrifices, but his determination paid off. Leo not only became the first in his family to graduate from college but went on to establish a successful career. His story is a testament to the power of education and the impact of perseverance.

Then there's Ava, who was raised in a family where she was constantly told that she would never amount to anything. Despite the lack of encouragement and support, Ava chose to believe in herself. She pursued her passion for art, often painting late into the night after her day job. Her persistence and belief in her own worth paid off. Today,

Ava is a renowned artist, her work celebrated for its vibrancy and depth. Her journey is a powerful reminder that the voices of doubt, whether from within or from others, can be silenced by self-belief and determination.

Another inspiring example is that of Sam. Born into a family with a history of substance abuse, Sam's early life was fraught with instability and challenges. Recognizing the destructive pattern, Sam made a conscious choice to break the cycle. He sought help, surrounded himself with positive influences, and dedicated himself to personal development. Today, Sam is not only living a life free of substance abuse but is also a counselor, helping others overcome their struggles. His story highlights the power of breaking negative cycles and the impact one individual can have on others.

These stories share a common thread – the refusal to let their upbringing dictate their future. They remind us that while we may not have control over the circumstances we are born into, we have the power to shape our future through our choices and actions. It's about recognizing that our past can inform us but doesn't have to confine us.

The stories of Leo, Ava, and Sam are shining examples of the incredible human capacity to transcend one's upbringing. They demonstrate that with resilience, belief in oneself, and the courage to make conscious choices, it is possible to rise above challenging beginnings and create a life of success and fulfillment. Let their stories be a source of inspiration, a reminder that no matter where you start, you have the power to chart your own course and achieve your dreams.

Crafting Your Story: Techniques for a Positive Personal Narrative

Your personal narrative is the story you tell yourself about who you are, where you've been, and where you're going. It's a powerful force that shapes your self-image, your choices, and ultimately, your life. This chapter is dedicated to helping you craft a positive personal narrative, one that empowers and uplifts you, allowing you to take control of your life's direction with confidence and optimism.

The first step in creating a positive personal narrative is recognizing the power of your current story. Every thought, every belief about yourself, is a thread in the tapestry of your narrative. Ask yourself: What story have I been telling myself? Is it one of triumph, resilience, and growth? Or is it a tale marred by self-doubt and perceived limitations? Acknowledging the narrative you've woven thus far is crucial in understanding how it has shaped your life.

Now, let's focus on rewriting the script. Start by identifying negative or limiting beliefs in your current narrative. Maybe it's a belief that you're not good enough, or that success is always just out of reach. Recognize that these beliefs are not truths; they're merely parts of an old story that you have the power to change.

The next step is reframing your past experiences. Look back at your challenges and setbacks. Instead of viewing them as failures or shortcomings, see them as stepping stones, lessons learned, and opportunities for growth.

Remember, it's not the events of your life that define you, but the meaning you attach to them. Take Marcus, for example, who saw his early career struggles not as failures but as essential experiences that taught him resilience and adaptability, shaping him into a successful entrepreneur.

Another technique is to practice positive self-talk. Your words have power, especially the ones you use to talk to yourself. Replace self-criticism with words of encouragement and affirmation. Make it a habit to acknowledge your strengths, celebrate your successes, and speak to yourself with kindness and respect.

Visualization is a powerful tool in crafting your narrative. Envision the future you desire. See yourself achieving your goals, living your dreams, and being the person you aspire to be. This visualization isn't mere daydreaming; it's setting the stage for your narrative to unfold.

It's also important to set goals and take action. Your narrative is not just about what you think or say; it's about what you do. Set small, achievable goals that align with your positive narrative. Each step you take towards these goals reinforces your new story.

Lastly, surround yourself with positivity. Seek out relationships and environments that support and reflect the narrative you want to live. Just as a negative environment can reinforce a negative narrative, a positive one can do the opposite.

Crafting a positive personal narrative is a powerful process of self-discovery and growth. It involves recognizing and reframing your past, practicing positive self-talk, visualizing your future, taking action towards your goals, and surrounding yourself with positivity. Remember, you are the author of your story. With each word, thought, and action, you have the power to write a narrative that uplifts, empowers, and propels you towards a life of fulfillment and success.

From Past to Promise: Exercises for a Brighter Tomorrow

Your past is a mosaic of experiences that have shaped you, but it's your actions today that will sculpt your future. This chapter introduces practical exercises designed to help you reconcile with your past and pave the way for a brighter, more fulfilling future. It's about learning from yesterday to thrive tomorrow, embracing the journey of personal growth with empowerment and resilience.

The first step in reconciling with your past is acknowledging it. This involves looking back at your experiences, both positive and negative, and accepting them as part of your story. One effective exercise for this is journaling. Write down the significant events of your past, the good and the bad. Describe how they made you feel, what you learned, and how they've influenced your present. This practice not only provides emotional release but also helps in understanding and accepting your past.

Once you've acknowledged your past, it's time to let go of any lingering negative emotions. A powerful exercise for this is the 'letter of release.' Write a letter to your past self or to someone who has hurt you. Pour out your feelings, express forgiveness, and then, symbolically let it go. You could tear it up, burn it (safely), or even just store it away. The act of releasing these emotions is a cathartic step towards healing and moving forward.

Next, focus on the lessons your past has taught you. Reflect on how each experience has contributed to your growth. You might find that challenges taught you resilience, mistakes led to wisdom, and heartaches brought strength. Acknowledging these lessons turns your past into a valuable resource for personal development.

Now, turn your attention to the future. One effective technique is goal-setting. Start by visualizing where you want to be in the next year, five years, or even ten years. What does this future look like? How are you living, feeling, and interacting with the world? Then, set specific, achievable goals that will guide you towards this vision. Break these goals down into smaller steps and start taking action, one day at a time.

Another key exercise is creating a vision board. Collect images, quotes, and symbols that represent your goals and aspirations. Arrange them on a board and place it somewhere you'll see it daily. This visual representation serves as a constant reminder and motivator for your journey towards a better future.

It's also important to cultivate a positive mindset. Practice gratitude by writing down three things you're grateful for each day. This shifts your focus from what's lacking to what's abundant, fostering a sense of optimism and well-being.

In conclusion, reconciling with your past and planning for a better future involves a blend of reflection, release, learning, visualization, goal-setting, and cultivating positivity. Remember, your past doesn't define you—it prepares you. Embrace these exercises as tools to help you learn from your history, let go of what no longer serves you, and step confidently into a future filled with promise and potential. Your journey from past to promise is a testament to your resilience and power to shape your destiny.

Chapter 13

Conclusion: Crafting a Positive Tomorrow

As we draw the curtains on this empowering journey, it's vital to remember that the narrative of your life is yours to write. Crafting a positive tomorrow is not about awaiting a stroke of luck or the perfect circumstances; it's about the choices you make every day, the small steps you take towards your goals, and the mindset with which you face life's challenges. This conclusion is a call to action – an invitation to embrace your power and craft a future brimming with positivity and fulfillment.

The journey to a positive tomorrow begins with a single step: the decision to take control of your life. Each day presents a new opportunity to make choices that align with your values and aspirations. It's about being proactive rather than reactive, making decisions that lead you closer to the life you envision. Remember, even the smallest choices can have a profound impact on your life trajectory.

One of the most powerful tools in your arsenal is the practice of positive thinking. It's not about ignoring life's challenges or painting a rosy picture of reality. Instead, it's about adopting a mindset that seeks solutions, finds silver linings, and focuses on growth and possibilities. Positive thinking empowers you to approach obstacles with a can-do attitude, transforming challenges into opportunities for growth.

Incorporate the habit of goal-setting into your daily life. Set clear, achievable goals for yourself, both short-term and long-term. Break these goals down into actionable steps and celebrate each milestone along the way. Remember, every achievement, no matter how small, is a step closer to your ideal tomorrow.

Reflect on your journey regularly. Take time to acknowledge your progress, learn from your experiences, and adjust your course as needed. Reflection is a powerful tool for growth, allowing you to pause, assess, and move forward with greater wisdom and clarity.

Cultivate resilience. Life will inevitably throw challenges your way, but your strength lies in how you respond to them. Resilience is about bouncing back from setbacks, learning from failure, and keeping going despite difficulties. It's the cornerstone of a positive tomorrow.

Surround yourself with positivity. Seek relationships and environments that uplift and support you. Surround yourself with people who inspire you, challenge you, and encourage your growth. Your environment plays a crucial role in shaping your mindset and your journey.

Finally, never underestimate the power of gratitude. Practice being grateful for the big and small things in your life. Gratitude shifts your focus from what you lack to what you have, fostering a sense of abundance and well-being. It's a key ingredient in crafting a positive and fulfilling tomorrow.

The path to a positive tomorrow is paved with the choices you make today. Embrace the power of positive thinking, goal-setting, reflection, resilience, positive environments, and gratitude. Your journey is unique, and every step you take shapes the narrative of your life. Remember, you have the power to craft a future filled with hope, happiness, and success. Here's to crafting your positive tomorrow – one choice, one step, one day at a time.

In "Shaping Tomorrow: The Power of Response Over Circumstance," we embark on a transformative journey, exploring the profound impact of personal power in shaping our lives. This book delves deep into the philosophy of personal empowerment, emphasizing the crucial role of mindset, decision-making, and resilience in overcoming life's challenges.

Chapter 1: The Philosophy of Personal Power

We begin by defining personal power and its significance in facing life's adversities. Through real-life case studies, we illustrate how our responses to external events, rather than the events themselves, shape our experiences. This section sets the stage for the book's exploration of mindset, control, and empowerment.

Chapter 2: The Legacy of a Troubled Past

Here, we address the challenges of a difficult upbringing and its impact on adult behavior and relationships. We explore strategies for healing and moving beyond a troubled past, supported by inspiring stories of individuals who have successfully navigated similar journeys.

Chapter 3: Beyond Blame: Owning Our Present

This chapter tackles the tendency to blame our upbringing for current issues, highlighting the importance of shifting from blame to empowerment. We introduce techniques for self-awareness and accountability, emphasizing the transformative power of owning our present.

Chapter 4: Wisdom from Wounds

Focusing on post-traumatic growth, we explore how adversity can be a source of learning and resilience.

Practical exercises are provided to help readers transform their painful experiences into wisdom and strength.

Chapter 5: Unique Challenges, Universal Choices

We discuss the diversity of individual challenges and the universal power of choice in responding to adversity. Strategies for making empowering choices are presented, along with stories of individuals who chose positivity in the face of difficulty.

Chapter 6: The Myth of Ideal Situations

This chapter challenges the pursuit of "perfect" circumstances, advocating for adaptability and resilience. We share real-life examples of thriving in less-than-ideal conditions and strategies for developing a realistic, positive outlook.

Chapter 7: The Trap of Self-Victimization

We delve into the psychology of self-victimization, discussing its impact on personal growth. Strategies for overcoming this mindset are explored, along with success stories of individuals who broke free from self-imposed victimhood.

Chapter 8: Learning from the Past, Shaping the Future

The importance of reflecting on the past to inform future growth is highlighted. We discuss forgiveness, letting go, and using past experiences as a foundation for future success, complemented by inspirational stories and guided activities.

Chapter 9: Beyond Complaints: Embracing Responsibility

This chapter examines the detrimental effects of habitual complaining, advocating for a shift to a solution-oriented mindset. Techniques for cultivating gratitude and positive thinking are introduced, along with transformations from chronic complainers to proactive individuals.

Chapter 10: Inner Strength in Adversity

We explore building emotional and mental fortitude to overcome adversity. Stories of individuals who found strength in challenging times are shared, along with strategies for maintaining composure and clarity in crises.

Chapter 11: The Conscious Choice

The power of conscious decision-making in shaping life experiences is emphasized. We explore differentiating between reactive and proactive responses and techniques for enhancing decision-making skills.

Chapter 12: The Role of Upbringing and Moving Forward

Analyzing the impact of upbringing on adult behavior and choices, we discuss balancing acknowledgment of the past with a focus on the future. Inspirational examples and techniques for creating a positive personal narrative are provided.

Chapter 13 Conclusion: Crafting a Positive Tomorrow

In the conclusion, we summarize the key insights and lessons from the book, reinforcing the message that the power to shape a positive tomorrow lies in our responses and choices today. This final chapter serves as a powerful reminder of the enduring strength and resilience inherent in each of us, guiding readers to a future filled with hope, growth, and empowerment.

Embracing Change: A Personal Message from Ine

Hello, I'm Ine, and I've shared this journey with you through the pages of our book. As we turn the final page, I want to encourage you, from the bottom of my heart, to apply the concepts we've explored together to your life. This isn't just a book; it's a toolkit for transformation, a companion in your journey towards a more empowered and fulfilling life.

Throughout our time together, we've delved into the power of decision-making and how even the smallest choices can significantly impact our life trajectory. I've shared stories of resilience and triumph, hoping to inspire and empower you. Now, the real work begins – it's your turn to take these lessons and weave them into the fabric of your life.

Remember, change doesn't happen overnight. It's a gradual process, a series of steps taken one day at a time. Start small. Choose one concept from the book that resonated deeply with you, and focus on incorporating it into your daily routine. Maybe it's practicing mindfulness, setting achievable goals, or shifting your mindset from blame to empowerment. Whatever it is, let it be the first stone in your path towards a brighter future.

I know from personal experience that change can be daunting. It's tempting to fall back into familiar patterns, even if they don't serve us well. But remember, every great journey begins with a single step. Take that step with courage and conviction. You have the power within you to shape your destiny, to break free from old patterns, and to create a life that reflects your true potential.

As you apply these concepts, be patient with yourself. Growth is not linear, and setbacks are a natural part of the process. What matters is not how many times you stumble, but how many times you rise. Each time you do, you'll be stronger and wiser than before.

Also, don't go it alone. Share your journey with others. Find support among friends, family, or a community of like-minded individuals. Their encouragement, perspectives, and experiences can be invaluable sources of strength and inspiration.

Most importantly, celebrate your progress, no matter how small it may seem. Every step forward is a victory, a testament to your commitment to personal growth. Acknowledge your efforts, cherish your achievements, and let them fuel your journey forward.

I want to express my deepest gratitude for allowing me to be a part of your journey. Remember, the lessons in this book are not just concepts to be read but lived. Embrace them, practice them, and let them guide you towards a life of empowerment, resilience, and fulfillment. Your future is a canvas of endless possibilities – grab that brush and paint a picture that resonates with your deepest aspirations. You have the power to shape a remarkable future, and I can't wait to see where your journey takes you.

The Journey of Endless Growth: Embracing Continuous Personal Development

Each thread we weave is a testament to our growth and evolution. Continuous personal development is not just a concept; it's a way of life, a commitment to becoming the best version of ourselves. This journey is about embracing change, learning from experiences, and applying those lessons to grow continuously.

The importance of continuous personal development cannot be overstated. In a world that is constantly evolving, staying stagnant is not an option. We need to adapt, learn, and grow to keep pace with the changes around us. This development isn't confined to professional skills; it encompasses personal growth, emotional intelligence, and resilience.

Think of life as a garden. Just as a garden requires regular care, watering, and pruning to flourish, our lives require ongoing attention and nurturing. Personal development is the water and sunlight of our garden, essential for growth and vitality. Without it, we risk becoming stagnant, withering under the unchanging sun of complacency.

Let me share a story that illustrates this point. Sarah, a friend of mine, felt stuck in her job. Every day was the same, and she felt her skills and passion slowly diminishing. It was only when she took the initiative to enroll in a course to enhance her skills and reignite her passion that she started to see a change. This step sparked a journey of personal development that not only transformed her career but also her personal life. Sarah's story is a testament to the transformative power of continuous learning and growth.

Continuous personal development is also crucial in building resilience. Life will inevitably throw challenges our way, and how we respond to these challenges defines our journey. By committing to personal growth, we equip ourselves with the tools to face adversity, learn from it, and emerge stronger. It's about turning obstacles into opportunities for growth.

Moreover, this journey fosters a deeper sense of self-awareness and fulfillment. As we learn and grow, we gain a better understanding of who we are, what we value, and what we aspire to achieve. This understanding is vital in living a life that is not only successful but also meaningful and fulfilling.

So, how do we embark on this journey of continuous personal development? It starts with a mindset of curiosity and openness to learning. Seek out new experiences, read widely, and embrace opportunities to learn from others. Set personal and professional goals, and take small, consistent steps towards achieving them. Reflect on your experiences, acknowledging both your successes and areas for improvement.

Remember, the journey of personal development is unique for each of us. There is no one-size-fits-all approach. It's about finding what works for you, whether it's taking courses, seeking mentorship, engaging in reflective practices, or pushing yourself out of your comfort zone.

Continuous personal development is an essential journey, a commitment to never stop growing. It's about embracing the idea that no matter how much we know, there's always more to learn, more to explore, and more ways to grow. This journey is not just about personal or professional success; it's about crafting a life of richness, depth, and fulfillment. So, let's keep growing, learning, and evolving, for the journey of personal development is truly endless.

Take the Helm: Your Call to Shape Your Future

As we get ready to close this chapter together, I want to leave you with more than just words on a page; I want to ignite a spark within you. This is your call to action, a rallying cry to seize the reins of your life and shape your future with intention and conviction. The journey ahead is yours to chart, and the time to start is now.

First, let's understand the incredible power of decision-making. Every decision, no matter how small, steers the course of your life. Think of it as setting the coordinates in your life's GPS. Sometimes, the changes might seem insignificant, like choosing a healthier meal or setting aside time for personal reflection. But these small choices add up, creating a trajectory that leads you towards a future you desire. The key is to make these decisions consciously, aligning them with your values and goals.

Reflect on your life as it is today. Are there aspects you wish to change? Areas you want to improve? Dreams you've shelved? Now is the time to dust off those dreams and take proactive steps towards making them a reality. It doesn't require monumental shifts; often, the most significant transformations stem from small, consistent actions.

I want to share a story about my friend, Alex. He felt trapped in a job that didn't fulfill him, dreaming of starting his own business. For years, he remained in his comfort zone, letting fear and uncertainty hold him back. The turning point came when he finally decided to take one small step - attending a workshop on entrepreneurship. That single action set off a chain of events that led to him successfully launching his business. This demonstrates the power of taking that first step, no matter how daunting it may seem.

Embracing this journey also means being prepared to face challenges and setbacks. Resilience is key. Remember, setbacks are not failures; they're opportunities to learn, grow, and come back stronger. When faced with obstacles, ask yourself, 'What can I learn from this?' Embrace the growth mindset that every experience, good or bad, is a stepping stone to your success.

Another crucial aspect is to surround yourself with positivity and support. Connect with people who inspire you, who challenge you to be your best self. Seek mentors, join communities, or even find accountability partners who share your aspirations. The people you surround yourself with can significantly influence your journey.

Finally, never forget the importance of self-care and reflection. In the pursuit of your goals, take time to care for your physical, emotional, and mental well-being. Reflect on your progress, celebrate your successes, and be kind to yourself during times of struggle.

This is your moment. Your future is a canvas awaiting your brushstrokes. Every choice you make, every action you take, paints a part of this vast mural. Dream big, start small, stay resilient, and take control of your story. Your future is not a matter of chance; it's a matter of choice. So, take the helm, set your course, and sail towards the horizon of your aspirations. The world awaits what you have to offer, and the journey starts with you.

Embracing the Journey: Reflections on Transformation and Growth

As we embark on the path of transformation and growth, it's vital to pause and reflect on the journey itself. This journey is not just about reaching a destination or achieving goals; it's about the profound changes we experience along the way, the challenges we overcome, and the invaluable lessons we learn. It's a journey marked by resilience, self-discovery, and empowerment.

Let's start by acknowledging that transformation is not a linear process. It's filled with highs and lows, successes and setbacks. Each step, whether forward or backward, is an integral part of your growth. Remember, it's in the ebb and flow of experiences that we find our strength and resilience. Just like a river that weathers both calm and stormy waters, our journey of transformation is dynamic and ever-evolving.

Think about the small changes you've made that have led to significant impacts in your life. Maybe it was the decision to wake up a little earlier each day to meditate or exercise, or perhaps it was choosing to read a book instead of watching television. These small changes often go unnoticed at the moment but, over time, they accumulate, leading to profound transformations.

I recall a friend, Emily, who felt overwhelmed by her hectic life. She started by making a small change: dedicating ten minutes each day to journaling. This simple practice helped her understand her thoughts and emotions better, leading to more significant changes in her life, like pursuing a career that aligned with her passion. Emily's story is a powerful reminder that transformation often begins with a single, small step.

The journey of transformation is also about self-discovery. It's a journey inward, exploring the depths of who we are, what we value, and what we aspire to be. It's about peeling back the layers, confronting our fears, and uncovering our true potential. This process can be challenging, but it's also incredibly rewarding. With each step forward, you gain a deeper understanding of yourself and a clearer vision of your life's purpose.

Moreover, this journey teaches us the importance of resilience. We learn to embrace failures not as endings but as opportunities to grow and learn. Each challenge we face and overcome fortifies our resilience, making us stronger and more adaptable. It's about adopting a mindset that views obstacles as stepping stones to success.

Lastly, transformation and growth are about empowerment. It's realizing that you have the power to shape your destiny. You are not a passive bystander in your life; you are the architect. By making conscious choices and taking deliberate actions, you shape the narrative of your life.

The journey of transformation and growth is a beautiful and complex tapestry woven from experiences, choices, and lessons. It's about embracing the process, celebrating the small victories, learning from setbacks, and continuously striving towards becoming the best version of yourself. Remember, this journey is uniquely yours. Own it, cherish it, and let it be a source of strength and inspiration. As you continue on your path, take pride in how far you've come, and look forward to the endless possibilities that lie ahead.

Final Thoughts: Mastering the Power of Response Over Circumstance

As we reach the conclusion of our journey together, it's essential to reflect on a fundamental truth that has been the heartbeat of our discussions: the incredible power of our response over our circumstances. This principle isn't just a concept; it's a transformative force that can reshape our lives. It's about understanding that while we cannot always control what happens to us, we have absolute power over how we respond.

The stories and principles shared in this book are testaments to the strength and resilience that lie within each of us. They serve as reminders that our responses to life's challenges can be our most powerful tools in crafting a life of fulfillment and success. Remember, it's not the events in our lives that define us, but rather how we choose to react to them.

Think about a time when you faced a difficult situation. How did you respond? Did you allow the circumstance to overwhelm you, or did you find strength and resilience within yourself? This reflection is crucial because it highlights a key aspect of our nature: our capacity to choose our response in any situation.

Let's take the example of Anna, who faced a career setback when she was unexpectedly laid off from her job. Initially, Anna felt defeated and lost. However, she soon realized that this setback was an opportunity to reassess her career path and explore new possibilities. By choosing to view her circumstance as a chance for growth, Anna opened the door to new opportunities that aligned more closely with her passions and skills. Her story illustrates that our power lies not in what happens to us, but in how we respond to it.

Embracing this power requires a mindset shift. It calls for us to move away from a mindset of victimhood, where we feel powerless against our circumstances, and towards a mindset of empowerment. It's about adopting an attitude of resilience and adaptability, understanding that challenges are not roadblocks but stepping stones on the path to growth and success.

Moreover, this approach to life empowers us to take control of our destiny. It frees us from the constraints of our circumstances and allows us to create our path. By focusing on our responses, we become the architects of our future, building it with the bricks of our choices and actions.

In conclusion, as we part ways, I urge you to carry with you the understanding that your power lies in your response. Life will undoubtedly present its challenges, but remember, each challenge is an opportunity to demonstrate your strength, resilience, and ability to rise above. Embrace every situation with a mindset of growth and empowerment. Let your responses be guided by your values, goals, and aspirations. Remember, you have the power to shape your life, not by the circumstances that befall you, but by the responses you choose. As you move forward, let this be your guiding principle, and watch as you transform challenges into opportunities, and dreams into realities.

"The last of human freedoms: to choose one's attitude in any given set of
circumstances, to choose one's own way."

Viktor E. Frankl, *Man's Search for Meaning*